S0-CMS-784

Order Form

The New E-Discovery Rules

Three easy ways to order:

- *Photocopy and fax:* this order form to 978-456-9247
- *Mail*: this order form to the address below.
- *Call*: 978-456-9042

Price Information:

Quantity	Unit Price
01 - 19	$15.00
20 - 49	12.50
50 - 99	10.00
100 - 249	9.00
250+	call

Order Information:

Total books _____ x $_____ (unit price) = total book price.........$_____

Shipping & handling (total book price x .08).....................................$_____

Sales tax (Massachusetts residents only; total book price x .05)..........$_____

Total amount of order ....$_____

Payment Method: ❑ Check   ❑ Visa   ❑ Mastercard

Card #: _____ Exp. _____

Printed Name: _____

Signature: _____

Card Billing Address _____
                    (Street Address & Zip Code only)

Shipping Information:

Name: _____

Firm: _____

Address: _____

City: _____

State: _____ Zip: _____ Phone: _____

Dahlstrom Legal Publishing, Inc., 113 E Bare Hill Rd, Harvard, MA 01451
www.legalpub.com

The New E-Discovery Rules:

Amendments to the Federal Rules of Civil Procedure Scheduled to Take Effect Dec. 1, 2006

Excerpts from the September 2005 Report
of the Committee on Rules of Practice & Procedure
and the May 2005 Report
of the Civil Rules Advisory Committee

Published by
Dahlstrom Legal Publishing, Inc.
Harvard, Massachusetts

© 2006 Dahlstrom Legal Publishing, Inc.
Harvard, Massachusetts

ALL RIGHTS RESERVED. Contents may not be reproduced, stored, or transmitted in any form or by any means, electronic or mechanical, including photocopying, recording, or by any information storage and retrieval system without permission in writing from the publisher. Copyright is not claimed as to any part of the original work prepared by a U.S. Government officer or employee as part of that person's official duties.

Printed and bound in the United States of America. ISBN: 0-9773729-2-8

The publisher has made every effort to ensure the accuracy of information contained in this product but cannot assume liability for inadvertent errors.

Comments and corrections are welcome and may be emailed to comments@legalpub.com. Corrections are posted on our website www.legalpub.com.

Dahlstrom Legal Publishing, Inc.
113 East Bare Hill Rd.
Harvard, MA 01451-1856
Tele: 1-978-456-9042
Fax: 1-978-456-9247
Web: www.legalpub.com

Preface

On May 27, 2005, the Advisory Committee on the Federal Rules of Civil Procedure submitted to the Standing Committee on the Rules of Practice and Procedure a comprehensive package of proposed amendments to the Federal Rules of Civil Procedure. The proposed amendments addressed discovery of electronically stored information and affected Rules 16(b), 26(a), 26(b)(2), 26(b)(5), 26(f), 33, 34(a), 34(b), 37(f) and 45, as well as Form 35. The proposals would revamp existing discovery rules in order to better accommodate discovery directed at information generated by computers. The Advisory Committee package included a historical analysis, a description of the efforts which led to the proposed amendments, a statement of each proposed rule change in "black line" format, as well as explanatory "Committee Notes."

On June 16, 2005, the Standing Committee on Rules of Practice and Procedure approved the package of proposed amendments without change. (Changes were made to some committee notes.) In September 2005, the Standing Committee submitted the package of proposed amendments to the Judicial Conference, along with a written report. On September 20, 2005, the Judicial Conference of the United States approved the package of amendments.

On April 12, 2006, the United States Supreme Court approved the entire package of proposed amendments without comment. The amendments will become effective on December 1, 2006, absent Congressional action to the contrary.

This publication includes portions of the September 2005 Standing Committee report and the May 27, 2005 Advisory Committee package pertaining to the amendments addressing discovery of electronically stored information. It also includes amendments to a number of non-discovery related federal rules of civil procedure which were also approved by the Supreme Court.

The Publisher
April 2006

Contents

Standing Committee Report

REPORT OF THE JUDICIAL CONFERENCE COMMITTEE ON RULES OF PRACTICE AND PROCEDURE TO THE CHIEF JUSTICE OF THE UNITED STATES AND MEMBERS OF THE JUDICIAL CONFERENCE OF THE UNITED STATES:*

The Committee on Rules of Practice and Procedure met on June 15-16, 2005. All members of the Committee attended as well as the Committee's reporter, Professor Daniel R. Coquillette. The Deputy Attorney General, James B. Comey, attended the meeting with John S. Davis, Associate Deputy Attorney General, and Elizabeth Shapiro, Assistant Director, Federal Programs Branch, Civil Division, Department of Justice. Professor Geoffrey C. Hazard and Joseph F. Spaniol, consultants to the Committee, and John K. Rabiej, Chief of the Administrative Office's Rules Committee Support Office also attended.

All of the chairs and reporters of the advisory rules committees were present, with the exception of the reporter to the Appellate Rules Committee, as follows: Judge Samuel A. Alito, chair of the Advisory Committee on Appellate Rules; Judge Thomas S. Zilly, chair, and Professor Jeffrey W. Morris, reporter, of the Advisory Committee on Bankruptcy Rules; Judge Lee H. Rosenthal, chair, and Professor Edward H. Cooper, reporter, of the Advisory Committee on Civil Rules; Judge Susan C. Bucklew, chair, and Professor David A. Schlueter, reporter, of the Advisory Committee on Criminal Rules; and Judge Jerry E. Smith, chair, and Professor Daniel J. Capra, reporter, of the Advisory Committee on Evidence Rules. Also in attendance were Professor Sara Sun Beale, consultant to the Criminal Rules Committee, James N. Ishida and Jeffrey N. Barr, attorney advisors in the Administrative Office, and Tim Reagan of the Federal Judicial Center.

* * * * *

FEDERAL RULES OF CIVIL PROCEDURE

Rules Recommended for Approval and Transmission

The Advisory Committee on Civil Rules submitted proposed amendments to Rules 16, 26, 33, 34, 37, 45, 50, Supplemental Rules A, C, and E, and a new Supplemental Rule G (with conforming amendments to Rules 9(h), 14, 26(a), and 65.1), and revisions to Form 35 with a recommendation that they be approved and transmitted to the Judicial Conference. The amendments were circulated to the bench and bar for comment in August 2004. Three public

---

*Publisher's note: The September 2005 report of the Committee on Rules of Practice and Procedure also addressed proposed amendments to non-discovery related federal rules of civil procedure as well as to other sets of court rules. The portion of the report set forth herein pertains only to those proposed amendments to the federal rules of civil procedure which address discovery of electronically stored information.

hearings were held at which 74 witnesses testified; many of these witnesses also submitted written comments. An additional 180 written comments were submitted.

Discovery of Electronically Stored Information

The proposed amendments to Rules 16, 26, 33, 34, 37, 45, and revisions to Form 35 are aimed at discovery of electronically stored information. The advisory committee first heard about problems with computer-based discovery at a discovery conference in 1996. In 1999, the then-chair laid out the advisory committee's daunting mission to devise "mechanisms for providing full disclosure in a context where potential access to information is virtually unlimited and in which full discovery could involve burdens far beyond anything justified by the interests of the parties to the litigation." The advisory committee began intensive work on this subject in 2000. Since then, bar organizations, attorneys, computer specialists, and members of the public have devoted much time and energy in helping the rules committees understand and address the serious problems arising from discovery of electronically stored information. The advisory committee's study included several mini-conferences and one major conference, bringing together lawyers, academics, judges, and litigants with a variety of experiences and viewpoints. The advisory committee also heard from experts in information technology who provide technical electronic discovery services to lawyers and litigants.

The discovery of electronically stored information raises markedly different issues from conventional discovery of paper records. Electronically stored information is characterized by exponentially greater volume than hardcopy documents. Commonly cited current examples of such volume include the capacity of large organizations' computer networks to store information in terabytes, each of which represents the equivalent of 500 million typewritten pages of plain text, and to receive 250 to 300 million e-mail messages monthly. Computer information, unlike paper, is also dynamic; merely turning a computer on or off can change the information it stores. Computers operate by overwriting and deleting information, often without the operator's specific direction or knowledge. A third important difference is that electronically stored information, unlike words on paper, may be incomprehensible when separated from the system that created it. These and other differences are causing problems in discovery that rule amendments can helpfully address.

The advisory committee monitored the experiences of the bar and bench with these issues for several years. It found that the discovery of electronically stored information is becoming more time-consuming, burdensome, and costly. The current discovery rules, last amended in 1970 to take into account changes in information technology, provide inadequate guidance to litigants, judges, and lawyers in determining discovery rights and obligations in particular cases. Developing case law on discovery into electronically stored information under the current rules is not consistent and is necessarily limited by the specific facts involved. Disparate local rules have emerged to fill this gap between the existing discovery rules and practice, and more courts are considering local rules. Without national rules adequate to address the issues raised by electronic discovery, a patchwork of rules and requirements is likely to develop. While such inconsistencies are particularly confusing and debilitating to large public and private organizations, the uncertainty, expense, delays, and burdens of such discovery also affect small organizations and even individual litigants.

The costs of complying with unclear and at times vague discovery obligations, which vary from district to district in ways unwarranted by local variations in practice, are becoming increasingly problematic. Unless timely action is taken to make the federal discovery rules better able to accommodate the distinctive features of electronic discovery, those rules will become increasingly removed from practice, and similarly situated litigants will continue to be treated differently depending on the federal forum.

Electronic Discovery in Historical Perspective

Before the civil rules became effective in 1938, discovery in both law and equity cases in the federal courts was extremely limited. The 1938 civil rules provided for liberal discovery, further expanded by amendments in 1946 and 1970. Since then, the discovery rules have been amended in 1980, 1983, 1993, and 2000 to provide more effective means for controlling overuse and occasional misuse of the discovery devices. Each of these proposed sets of discovery amendments was vigorously opposed both by those who perceived any narrowing of discovery as inimical to the basic premise of American litigation, and by those who protested that the rules committees had not gone far enough to control discovery and the attendant costs and delays. The present proposals have prompted similar reactions.

The present electronic discovery proposals grew out of the advisory committee's work on the 2000 amendments, which focused on the "architecture of discovery rules" to determine whether changes could be effected to reduce the costs of discovery, to increase its efficiency, to increase uniformity of practice, and to encourage the judiciary to participate more actively in case management when appropriate. The proposed amendments to make the rules apply better to electronic discovery problems share the same focus.

The historical perspective shows that any proposal to add or strengthen rule provisions for discovery containment produces significant debate. Such debate is not in itself a sign that the proposals are fundamentally flawed. It is right to be concerned if the proposals are supported only by a narrow segment of the bench or bar. But it is not surprising to find that proposals to increase judicial involvement in discovery or to encourage the application of the existing proportionality factors — which require a court to limit discovery if the costs and burdens outweigh its likely benefits — would be opposed more by one side of the bar than the other.

In general, there is a high level of support for rules changes to recognize and accommodate electronic discovery. The American Bar Association Section on Litigation, the Federal Bar Council, and the New York State Bar Association Commercial and Federal Litigation Section, all submitted comments generally supporting the proposed electronic discovery amendments and made helpful criticisms during the public comment period. The Department of Justice, which both brings and defends civil actions, also favors the proposals. To achieve yet a larger consensus, specific aspects of the published proposal that had been criticized during the public comment period were revised.

The advisory committee unanimously approved the amendments proposed to Rules 16, 26(a), 26(b)(5), 26(f), 33, 34, and Form 35. All but two members of the advisory committee voted in favor of recommending approval of the amendments to Rule 37(f) and Rule 26(b)(2), including the parallel provisions in the proposed amendment to Rule 45. The Committee supported all but two of the proposed amendments unanimously. The only exceptions were the proposed amendments to Rule 26(b)(5) and the parallel provisions in the proposed amendment to Rule 45, as to which four members withheld their support, and the proposed amendment to Rule 37(f), as to which one member abstained. The Committee Note has been revised to address certain of the concerns raised about Rule 26(b)(5).

Proposed Amendments to Rules 16, 26(a), 26(f), 33, 34, 45, and Form 35

The proposed amendments to Rule 16, Rule 26(a) and (f), and Form 35 present a framework for the parties and the court to give early attention to issues relating to electronic discovery, including the frequently-recurring problems of the preservation of evidence and the assertion of privilege and work-product protection.

The amendment to Rule 16 is designed to alert the court to the possible need to address the handling of discovery of electronically stored information early in the litigation, if such discovery is expected to occur. Rule 16 is amended to invite the court to address the disclosure or discovery of electronically stored information in the Rule 16 scheduling order. The amendment also gives the court discretion to enter an order adopting any agreements the parties reach for asserting claims of privilege or protection as trial-preparation material after inadvertent production in discovery.

Standing Committee Report

The proposed amendment to Rule 26(a) clarifies a party's duty to include in its initial disclosures electronically stored information by substituting "electronically stored information" for "data compilations." The amendment makes the rule consistent with disclosure practices in the courts and with the proposed electronic discovery amendment. It was not published for public comment and is recommended as a conforming amendment.

Under the proposed amendment to Rule 26(f), the parties' conference is to include discussion of any issues relating to disclosure or discovery of electronically stored information. The topics to be discussed include the form of producing electronically stored information, a distinctive and recurring problem in electronic discovery resulting from the fact that, unlike paper, electronically stored information may exist and be produced in a number of different forms. The parties are to discuss preservation, which has new importance in this context because of the dynamic character of electronic information. The parties are also directed to discuss whether they can agree on approaches to asserting claims of privilege or work-product protection after inadvertent production in discovery.

The problems that can result from efforts to guard against privilege waiver often become more acute when discovery of electronically stored information is sought. The volume of the information and the forms in which it is stored may make privilege determinations more difficult and privilege review correspondingly more expensive and time-consuming, yet less likely to detect all privileged information. Inadvertent production is increasingly likely to occur. Because the failure to screen out even one privileged item may result in an argument that there has been a waiver as to all other privileged materials related to the same subject matter, early attention to this problem is more important as electronic discovery becomes more common. Under the proposed amendments to Rules 26(f) and 16, if the parties are able to reach an agreement to adopt protocols for asserting privilege and work-product protection claims that will facilitate discovery that is faster and at lower cost, they may ask the court to include such arrangements in a case-management or other order.

The proposed amendments to Rules 33 and 34 clarify how these discovery workhorses are to apply to electronically stored information. The proposed amendment to Rule 33 clarifies that a party may answer an interrogatory involving review of business records by providing access to the information if the interrogating party can find the answer as readily as the responding party can.

Under the proposed amendment to Rule 34, electronically stored information is explicitly recognized as a category subject to discovery that is distinct from "documents" and "things." The term "documents" should not continue to be stretched to accommodate all the differences between paper and electronically stored information. Distinguishing in the rules between documents and electronically stored information makes it clear that there are differences between them important to managing discovery. Rule 34 is also amended to authorize a requesting party to specify the form of production, such as in paper or electronic form, and for the responding party to object. The rule provides an electronic discovery analogue to the existing language that prevents massive "dumps" of disorganized documents by requiring production of documents as they are ordinarily maintained or labeled to correspond with the categories in the request. Under the proposed amended rule, absent a court order, party agreement, or a request for a specific form for production, a party may produce responsive electronically stored information in the form in which the party ordinarily maintains it or in a reasonably usable form. Absent a court order, the party need only produce the same electronically stored information in one form.

The proposed amendment to Rule 45 conforms the provisions for subpoenas to changes in other discovery rules related to discovery of electronically stored information.

Form 35 is amended to add the parties' proposals regarding disclosure or discovery of electronically stored information to the list of topics to be included in the parties' report to the court.

The Committee concurred with the advisory committee's recommendations.

Recommendation: That the Judicial Conference approve the proposed amendments to Civil Rules 16, 26(a), 26(f), 33, 34, 45, and Form 35 and transmit them to the Supreme Court for its consideration with a recommendation that they be adopted by the Court and transmitted to Congress in accordance with the law.

Proposed Amendment to Rule 26(b)(5)

The proposed amendment to Rule 26(b)(5) provides a procedure for asserting privilege after production that is parallel to the similar proposals for Rules 16 and 26(f). As noted in describing Rules 16 and 26(f), the volume of electronically stored information searched and produced in response to discovery can be enormous, and certain features of the forms in which such information is stored make it more difficult to review for privilege and work-product protection than paper. The inadvertent production of privileged or protected material is a substantial risk. The proposed amendment to Rule 26(b)(5) clarifies the procedure to apply when a responding party asserts a claim of privilege or of work-product protection after production.

Standing Committee Report

Under the proposed amendment, if a party has produced information in discovery that it claims is privileged or protected as trial-preparation material, it may notify the receiving party of the claim, stating the basis for it. After receiving notification, the receiving party must return, sequester, or destroy the information, and may not use or disclose it to third parties until the claim is resolved. If the receiving party disclosed the information before being notified, the receiving party also must take reasonable steps to retrieve the information. The receiving party has the option of submitting the information directly to the court to decide whether the information is privileged or protected as claimed and, if so, whether a waiver has occurred. A producing party is not free to give belated notice of privilege or protection at any point in the litigation; courts will continue to examine whether a privilege or work-product protection claim was made at a reasonable time when delay is part of the substantive law on waiver.

Because the proposed amendment only establishes a procedure for asserting privilege or work-product protection claims after production and does not attempt to change the rules that determine whether production waives the privilege or protection asserted, it does not trigger the special statutory process for adopting rules that modify privilege. By providing a clear procedure to allow the responding party to assert privilege after production, the amendment helpfully addresses the parties' burden of privilege review, which is particularly acute in electronic discovery.

The proposed amendment to Rule 26(b)(5) did not attract controversy or much comment during the public comment period. However, it was the occasion of considerable debate at the Committee meeting. The four members who voted against the amendment to Rule 26(b)(5) expressed the view that the new procedure could be used to disrupt litigation, particularly if the claim of privilege or work-product was made late in the case. The majority of the Committee did not share the concern that parties would deliberately delay a claim of privilege or work product because to do so might waive the protection under the applicable substantive law. Moreover, bad faith litigation tactics are subject to sanctions and control by the court.

The Committee concurred with the advisory committee's recommendation.

Recommendation: That the Judicial Conference approve the proposed amendment to Civil Rule 26(b)(5) and transmit it to the Supreme Court for its consideration with a recommendation that it be adopted by the Court and transmitted to Congress in accordance with the law.

Proposed Amendment to Rule 26(b)(2)

The proposed amendment to Rule 26(b)(2) clarifies the obligations of a responding party to provide discovery of electronically stored information that is not reasonably accessible, an increasingly disputed aspect of such discovery. Under the amendment, a party need not produce electronically stored information that is not reasonably accessible because of undue burden or cost. While the features that may make it burdensome or costly to access electronically stored information vary from system to system and with the progress of electronic storage systems over time, examples under current technology include deleted information, information kept on some backup-tape systems for disaster recovery purposes, and legacy data remaining from systems no longer in use.

The amendment requires the responding party to identify the sources of potentially responsive information that it has not searched or produced because of the costs and burdens of accessing the information. This is an improvement over the present practice, in which responding parties simply do not produce electronically stored information that is difficult to access. Under the amended rule, if the requesting party moves for the production of such information, the responding party has the burden to show that the information is not reasonably accessible. Even if the responding party makes this showing, a court may order discovery for good cause and may impose appropriate terms and conditions. The proposed amendment codifies the best practices of parties and courts with experience in these issues.

The proposed amendment to Rule 26(b)(2) responds to distinctive problems encountered in discovery of electronically stored information that have no close analogue in the more familiar discovery of paper documents. Although computer storage often facilitates discovery, some forms of computer storage make it very difficult to access, search for, and retrieve information. The difficulties may arise for a number of different reasons primarily related to the technology of information storage, reasons that are likely to change over time. The information contained on easily accessed sources — whether computer-based, paper, or human — may be all that is reasonably useful or necessary for the litigation, particularly given the voluminous amounts of information characteristically available on computers. Lawyers sophisticated in these problems are developing a two-tier practice in which they first obtain and examine the information that can be provided from easily accessed sources and then determine whether it is necessary to search the difficult-to-access sources.

The relationship between the proposed rule and preservation is specifically addressed in the Committee Note, which states that the rule does not undermine or reduce common-law or statutory preservation obligations. A party is reminded that it may be obliged to preserve information stored on sources it has identified as not reasonably accessible, but the amendment does not attempt to define, and does not change, the preservation obligations that arise from independent sources of law. The amended rule requires that the information identified as not reasonably accessible must be difficult to access by the producing party for all purposes. A party that makes information "inaccessible" because it is likely to be discoverable in litigation is subject to sanctions now and would still be subject to sanctions under the proposed amendment.

The Committee concurred with the advisory committee's recommendation.

Recommendation: That the Judicial Conference approve the proposed amendment to Civil Rule 26(b)(2) and transmit it to the Supreme Court for its consideration with a recommendation that it be adopted by the Court and transmitted to Congress in accordance with the law.

Proposed Amendment to Rule 37(f)

The proposed amendment to Rule 37(f) responds to a distinctive and necessary feature of computer systems — the recycling, overwriting, and alteration of electronically stored information that attends normal use. This is a different problem from that presented by information kept in the static form that paper represents; such information is not destroyed without an affirmative, conscious effort. By contrast, computer systems lose, alter, or destroy information as part of routine operations, making the risk of losing information significantly greater than with paper. Even when litigation is anticipated, it can be very difficult to interrupt or suspend the routine operation of computer systems to isolate and preserve discrete parts of the information they overwrite, delete, or update on an ongoing basis, without creating problems for the larger system. Routine cessation or suspension of these features of computer operation is also undesirable; the result would be even greater accumulation of duplicative and irrelevant data that must be reviewed, making discovery more expensive and time-consuming. At the same time, a litigant's right to obtain evidence must be protected. There is considerable uncertainty as to whether a party must, at risk of severe sanctions, interrupt the operation of the electronic information systems it is using to avoid any loss of information because of the possibility that the information might be sought in discovery. The advisory committee has heard strong arguments in support of better guidance in the rules.

The proposed amendment provides limited protection against sanctions under the rules for a party's failure to provide electronically stored information in discovery. The proposed amendment states that absent exceptional circumstances, sanctions may not be imposed under the civil rules if electronically stored information sought in discovery has been lost as a result of the routine operation of an electronic information system, as long as that operation is in good faith. The proposed rule recognizes that all electronic information systems are designed to recycle, overwrite, and change information in routine operation, not because of any relationship between the content of particular information and litigation, but because they are necessary functions of regular business operations. The proposed rule also recognizes that suspending or interrupting these features can be prohibitively expensive and burdensome, again in ways that have no counterpart in managing hard-copy information. Using an example from current technology, many large organizations routinely recycle hundreds of backup tapes every two or three weeks; placing a hold on the recycling of these tapes for even short periods can result in hundreds of thousands of dollars of expense. Similarly, the regular purging of e-mails or other electronic communications is necessary to prevent a build-up of data that can overwhelm the most robust electronic information systems.

Systems must also be able to filter other types of communications in order to continue operations. Sophisticated and often custom-designed databases may be functional only if they continually revise the information they manage. Such information destruction features are an integral part of computer system design and operation. The amended rule applies only to information lost due to the "routine operation of an electronic information system" — the ways in which such systems are generally designed and programmed to meet the party's technical and business needs.

Sanctions are not avoided simply by showing that information was lost in the routine operation of an information system. It also must be shown that the operation was in good faith. The proposed amendment does not provide a shield for a party that intentionally destroys specific information because of its relationship to litigation, or for a party that allows such information to be destroyed in order to make it unavailable in discovery by exploiting the routine operation of an information system. Depending on the circumstances, good faith may require that a party intervene to modify or suspend certain features of the routine operation of a computer system to prevent the loss of information, if that information is subject to a preservation obligation. When such a preservation obligation arises depends on the substantive law of each jurisdiction, which is not affected by the proposed rule. If a party is under a duty to preserve information because of pending or reasonably anticipated litigation, such intervention in the routine operation of an informational system is one aspect of what is often called a "litigation hold."

By stating that, absent exceptional circumstances, sanctions may not be imposed under the discovery rules for electronically stored information lost because of the routine good faith operation of a computer system, the proposed rule provides guidance in a troublesome area distinctive to electronic discovery.

The Committee concurred with the advisory committee's recommendation.

Standing Committee Report

Recommendation: That the Judicial Conference approve the proposed amendment to Civil Rule 37(f) and transmit it to the Supreme Court for its consideration with a recommendation that it be adopted by the Court and transmitted to Congress in accordance with the law.

*****

The proposed amendments to the Federal Rules of Civil Procedure are in Appendix C with an excerpt from the advisory committee report.

Advisory Committee Report

To: **Honorable David F. Levi, Chair, Standing Committee on Rules of Practice and Procedure**

From: **Honorable Lee H. Rosenthal, Chair, Advisory Committee on the Federal Rules of Civil Procedure**

Date: **May 27, 2005 (Revised July 25, 2005)**

Re: **Report of the Civil Rules Advisory Committee**

Introduction

The Civil Rules Advisory Committee held three hearings in 2005 on proposed rules amendments published for comment in August 2004. The hearings were held on January 12 in San Francisco, January 28 in Dallas, and February 11 and 12 in Washington, D.C. The Committee met at the Administrative Office of the United States Courts on April 14-15, 2005. Draft minutes of the April 2005 meeting are attached. Summaries of the written comments and testimony presented at the hearings are also provided with the several recommendations of proposed rule amendments for adoption.

Parts I and II present action items. Part I recommends transmission for approval of amendments to several rules. Rules 5(e) and 50(b) come first. The next set of rule amendments is a comprehensive package addressing discovery of electronically stored information, including revisions of Rules 16, 26, 33, 34, 37, and 45, as well as Form 35. The last set of rule amendments recommended for approval is a new Supplemental Rule G governing civil forfeiture actions; this package includes conforming changes to other Supplemental Rules, including the title and Rules A, C, and E. Part I includes a conforming amendment to Rule 26(a)(1) that was published with Rule G and conforming amendments to Rules 9(h) and 14 and 26(a)(1)(E) that are recommended for adoption without publication. For each of the four categories of rule amendments recommended for approval, these materials set out a brief introductory discussion, followed by the text of the proposed rule amendment and Committee Note and a summary and explanation of the changes made since publication.[*]

* * * * *

C. Rules 16, 26, 33, 34, 37, 45, and Form 35
1.   Introduction

Over five years ago, the Advisory Committee began examining whether the discovery rules could better accommodate discovery directed at

---

[*]Publisher's note: The portion of the Advisory Committee report which addresses proposed amendments to non-discovery related federal rules of civil procedure is set forth at the end of this publication beginning on page 90.

Advisory Committee Report

information generated by, stored in, retrieved from, and exchanged through, computers. The proposed amendments published for comment in August 2004 resulted from an extensive and intensive study of such discovery. That study included several mini-conferences and one major conference, bringing together lawyers, academics, judges, and litigants with a variety of experiences and viewpoints. The Committee also sought out experts in information technology and heard from those involved in the rapidly expanding field of providing electronic discovery services to lawyers and litigants.

Through this study, the Committee reached consensus on two points. First, electronically stored information has important differences from information recorded on paper. The most salient of these differences are that electronically stored information is retained in exponentially greater volume than hard-copy documents; electronically stored information is dynamic, rather than static; and electronically stored information may be incomprehensible when separated from the system that created it. Second, these differences are causing problems in discovery that rule amendments can helpfully address.

In August 2004, the Committee published five categories of proposed amendments: amending Rules 16 and 26(f) to provide early attention to electronic discovery issues; amending Rule 26(b)(2) to provide better management of discovery into electronically stored information that is not reasonably accessible; amending Rule 26(b)(5) to add a new provision setting out a procedure for assertions of privilege after production; amending Rules 33 and 34 to clarify their application to electronically stored information; and amending Rule 37 to add a new section to clarify the application of the sanctions rules in a narrow set of circumstances distinctive to the discovery of electronically stored information. In addition, Rule 45 was to be amended to adapt it to the changes made in Rules 26-37.

At the three public hearings held in 2005, 74 witnesses testified, many of whom also submitted written comments. An additional 180 written comments were submitted. The Committee revised the proposed rules amendments and note language in light of the public comments. The Committee unanimously recommends that the Standing Committee approve the proposed amendments to Rules 16, 26(b)(5)(B), 26(f), 33, 34, 45, and Form 35, as well as a conforming amendment to Rule 26(a). All but two members of the Committee voted in favor of recommending that the Standing Committee approve the proposed amendments to Rules 26(b)(2) and 37(f). The Committee unanimously recommends that the Standing Committee approve the corresponding changes to Rule 45 except for the change that tracks proposed Rule 26(b)(2), and all but two members of the Committee recommend that the Standing Committee approve this portion of proposed amendment Rule 45. This introduction sets out a brief background of the Committee's work and discusses each of the proposed amendments.

When the 2000 amendments were in their early stages of consideration, it was very helpful to step back and consider what brought the Committee to that point. In a 1997 conference held at Boston College Law School – a meeting very similar in purpose to the 2003 conference on electronic discovery held at the Fordham University School of Law – Professors Stephen Subrin and Richard Marcus presented papers on the historical background of the discovery rules. Some highlights of their papers usefully put the present issues into perspective and context.

Before the civil rules became law in 1938, discovery in both law and equity cases in the federal courts had been extremely limited. When the Committee deliberated on the liberal discovery rules that Professor Edson Sunderland drafted, they raised the concern that expanded discovery would force settlements for reasons and on terms that related more to the costs of discovery than to the merits of the case, a concern raised frequently in the context of electronic discovery.[*] But the debates did not focus on discovery. Instead, the focus was on issues of national uniformity and separation of powers.

In 1946 and 1970, amendments to the discovery rules continued to expand the discovery devices. The 1970 amendments were what Professor Marcus has called the high-water mark of "party-controlled discovery."[**] Those amendments included the elimination of the requirement for a motion to obtain document production and of the good cause standard for document production. Since the "high-water mark," the discovery rules have been amended in 1980, 1983, 1993, and 2000, to provide more effective means for controlling the discovery devices. In 1980, the Committee made the first change designed to increase judicial supervision over discovery, adding a provision that allowed counsel to seek a discovery conference with the court. The Committee considered, and rejected, a proposal to narrow the scope of discovery from "relevant to the subject matter" to "relevant to the issues raised by the claims or defenses," and to limit the number of interrogatories. The public comment that proposal generated was similar in tone and in approach to some of the comments on certain of the electronic discovery proposals published in August 2004. Many protested any narrowing of discovery as inimical to the basic premise of American litigation; others protested that the Committee had not gone far enough in restricting discovery and controlling the costs and delay it caused; yet others worried that the Committee would feel "pressure" to approve rules prematurely.[***] In the face of the vigorous debate, the Committee withdrew these proposals and submitted what then-chair Judge Walter Mansfield characterized as "watered down" proposals. The scope change rejected

---

[*] Subrin, Fishing Expeditions Allowed: The Historical Background of the 1938 Federal Discovery Rules, 39 Boston Coll. L. Rev. 691, 730 (1998).

[**] Marcus, Discovery Containment Redux, 39 Boston Coll. L. Rev. 747, 749 (1998).

[***] Marcus, 39 Boston Coll. L. Rev. at 770.

Advisory Committee Report

in 1980 did become law, but not until 2000, and then in a modification that emphasized the supervisory responsibility of the court.

Despite an institutional bias against frequent rule changes, the lack of meaningful amendments in 1980 resulted in significant amendments three years later. The 1983 amendments marked a significant shift toward greater judicial involvement in all pretrial preparation, most particularly in the discovery process. The amendments expanded Rule 16 case-management orders; deleted the final sentence of Rule 26(a), which had said that "[u]nless the court orders otherwise under subdivision (c) of this rule, the frequency and use of these methods is not limited"; and added the paragraph to Rule 26(b) directing the court to limit disproportionate discovery. The newly-appointed reporter to the Advisory Committee, Professor Arthur Miller, described these changes as a "180 degree shift in orientation." Yet, as Professor Miller pointed out in his written submission to the Committee endorsing the proposed electronic discovery amendments, the 1983 amendments turned out not to be effective by themselves to calibrate the amount of discovery to the needs of particular cases.[*]

In 1993, continued unhappiness about discovery costs and related litigation delays led to a package of proposals that included mandatory broad initial disclosures (with a local rule opt-out feature added in response to vigorous criticism) and presumptive limits on the number of interrogatories and depositions. In part, these amendments were "designed to give teeth to the proportionality provisions added in 1983."[**] In 2000, the initial disclosure obligations were cut back and made uniform, and Rule 26(b)(1) was changed to limit the scope of party-controlled discovery to matters "relevant to the claim or defense of any party," allowing discovery into "the subject matter involved in the action" only on court order for good cause.

During the study that led to the 2000 amendments, the Advisory Committee became aware of problems relating to electronic discovery. The Committee was urged by lawyers, litigants, and a number of organized bar groups to examine these problems. In 1999, when the 2000 proposals were recommended for adoption following the public comment period, the Committee fully understood that its work was incomplete. In his 1999 report to the Standing Committee recommending adoption of the 2000 amendments, Judge Niemeyer observed that since the work on the proposals had begun in 1996, "the Committee . . . kept its focus on the long-range discovery issues that will confront it in the emerging information age. The Committee recognized that it will be faced with the task of devising mechanisms for providing full disclosure in a context where potential access to information is virtually unlimited and in which full discovery could involve burdens far beyond any-

---

[*]Prof. Arthur Miller, 04-cv-221.

[**]Marcus, Discovery Containment, 39 Boston Coll. L. Rev. at 766.

Advisory Committee Report

thing justified by the interests of the parties to the litigation. While the tasks of designing discovery rules for an information age are formidable and still face the Committee, the mechanisms adopted in the current proposals begin the establishment of a framework in which to work." The present electronic discovery proposals grow out of the Committee's work on the 2000 amendments and in many ways continue that work. As noted in the report to the Standing Committee in 1999, the Committee's efforts leading to the 2000 amendments focused on the "architecture of discovery rules" to determine whether changes can be effected to reduce the costs of discovery, to increase its efficiency, to increase uniformity of practice, and to encourage the judiciary to participate more actively in case management. The proposed amendments to make the rules apply better to electronic discovery problems have the same focus.

The historical perspective is a reminder that any proposal to add or strengthen rule provisions for what Professor Marcus calls "discovery containment" produces significant debate. The vigor, volume, and themes of the public comment on the August 2004 electronic discovery proposals are not new to proposed discovery rule amendments. The debates over the amendments that became effective in 1983, 1993, and 2000 were vigorous, with many favoring liberal party-controlled discovery and many advocating more effective tools for discovery management and limits. Such debate is not in itself a sign that the proposals are fundamentally flawed. It is right to be concerned if the proposals are only supported by a narrow segment of the bench or bar. But it is not surprising to find that proposals to increase judicial involvement in discovery or to encourage the application of the existing proportionality factors would be opposed more by one side of the bar than the other.

Without understating the nature or depth of the concerns raised in response to specific proposals, discussed at length below, it is useful to note some points of agreement. There was a high level of support for changes to the federal rules to recognize and accommodate electronic discovery. Although there was certainly disagreement as to the proposed amendments to Rules 26(b)(2) and 37(f), there was also support from broad-based organizations that do not represent a reflexive plaintiff or defense view, such as the American Bar Association Section of Litigation,[*] the Federal Bar Council,[**] and the New York State Bar Association Commercial and Federal Litigation Section.[***] Many of the comments criticized aspects of the published proposals that have now been revised. As noted, after the comment period, all but two members of the Advisory Committee approved these proposed amendments as revised in light of the comments. The proposals calling for early attention to electronic discovery

[*]04-cv-062.
[**]04-cv-191.
[***]04-cv-045.

23

Advisory Committee Report

and addressing problems in the form of producing electronically stored information received broad support from the bar and the unanimous approval of the Advisory Committee.

The historical review also provides a useful context for considering the question of timing. The Advisory Committee has a history of carefully considering rule amendments and, when appropriate, withdrawing proposed amendments after public comment. The class action proposals of 1996 are a good example. The history of discovery amendments in particular shows great caution. The most prominent example is the 1978 decision to defer the "scope" proposal because there was vigorous opposition, as well as vigorous support. That decision to defer was criticized on the ground that it would significantly delay the proposal. A version of the scope limitation did become effective – twenty years later. It is always tempting to defer action because more time brings more information, particularly in an area of ongoing technological change. But deferring has costs. The calendar of the rules enabling process makes any delay a significant one. As long ago as the 1998-99 hearings on what became the discovery amendments of 2000, lawyers were urging the Committee to proceed with alacrity in rulemaking for e-discovery. The need for rulemaking now in this area is reflected in the local rules and state rules that have been enacted and the growing number of such rules that have been proposed. Many of these local rule efforts have been deferred because of the proposals to amend the national rules, but the perceived need for such rules means that they will not remain in check indefinitely. The 1993 amendments led in part to the 2000 amendments, teaching us much about the problems of local rulemaking in areas that the national discovery rules address, problems that we do not want to create in the area of electronic discovery. And the possibility of technological change will always exist; there is no reason to think that stability on that front will arrive any time soon.

The Committee has been studying electronic discovery for the last five years. We have learned a great deal, reflected in the rule proposals and the refinements made since publication. Those proposals and refinements are summarized below.

2. The Specific Proposals

i. Early Attention to Electronic Discovery Issues: Rules 16, 26(a), 26(f), and Form 35

Introduction

The comments consistently applauded the directives in Rule 16(b) and Rule 26(f) for the parties to discuss electronically stored information in cases that involve such discovery and to include these topics in the report to the court, and for the court to include these topics in its scheduling orders. The overall directive is broad, but specific provisions focus on three areas recognized as frequent sources of difficulty in electronic discovery: the form of producing electronically stored information in discovery; preserving information for the litigation; and the assertion of privilege and work-product protection claims.

The proposed amendments that direct early attention to electronic discovery issues, as published, did not include a revision to Rule 26(a)(1), although the amendments to Rule 26(f) referred to disclosures as well as discovery of electronically stored information. The Committee approved a proposed conforming amendment to Rule 26(a), making the Rule 26(a)(1) description of information subject to disclosure requirements consistent with the addition of electronically stored information to the discovery rules. Present Rule 26(a)(1) is redundant in requiring disclosure of both certain "documents" and "data compilations," because the present version of Rule 34 makes "data compilation" a subset of "documents." Present Rule 26(a)(1) is potentially inconsistent with the proposed revision of Rule 34, which adds "electronically stored information" as a category separate from "documents." Amending Rule 26(a)(1) to make it apply to "documents and electronically stored information," and deleting the words "data compilations," cures this inconsistency. Because Rule 34(a) is revised to distinguish between "documents" and "electronically stored information," revising Rule 26(a)(1) to conform to this distinction removes the argument that there is a duty to provide in discovery, but not to disclose, electronically stored information.

One concern initially raised about adding electronically stored information to Rule 26(a)(1) was that it could require parties to locate and review such information too early in the case. Such information, often voluminous and dispersed, can be burdensome to locate and review, and early in the case the parties may not be able to identify with precision the information that will be called for in discovery. The Committee concluded that this concern was not an argument against this conforming amendment. The disclosure obligation has been read as applying to electronically stored information and will continue to apply. The obligation does not force a premature search, but only requires disclosure, either initially or by way of supplementation, of information that the disclosing party has decided it may use to support its case.

The Committee decided against revising Rule 26(a)(3) to include "electronically stored information." Rule 26(a)(3) applies "in addition to the disclosures required by Rule 26(a)(1)" and is directed to identifying exhibits for trial. Electronically stored information is included in "each document or other exhibit" that the current rule requires to be identified in pretrial disclosures.

Advisory Committee Report

Proposed amended Rule 26(f) states that the parties are to discuss "any issues relating to preserving discoverable information." Some comments urged that this directive should be downgraded to the Note, in part out of concern that calling for discussion of the question will promote early applications for preservation orders. Most comments supported the inclusion of preservation as a topic to be discussed early in the case. The dynamic nature of electronically stored information, and the fact that routine operation of computer systems changes and deletes information, make it important to address preservation issues early in cases involving discovery of such information. The Committee decided not to change the published rule language, which includes not only electronically stored information but all forms of information. In response to the concerns raised in the comment period about preservation orders, the Note has been revised to state that preservation orders entered over objections should be narrowly tailored and that preservation orders should rarely be issued on ex parte applications.

Proposed new Rule 26(f)(3) directs parties to discuss "any issues relating to disclosure or discovery of electronically stored information, including the form or forms in which it should be produced." Form 35 is amended to provide that in the report to the court of their proposed discovery plan, the parties include their proposals for disclosure or discovery of electronically stored information. Rule 16(b)(5) provides that the scheduling order the court enters may include "provisions for disclosure or discovery of electronically stored information." The comments emphasized the importance of discussing these topics early in the case, to identify disputes before costly and time-consuming searches and production occur. Only one change is proposed to this part of the published proposals. Many comments noted that more than one form of production might be appropriate in a case, because a party may store different information in different forms. Accordingly, this proposed amendment is revised to state that the parties should discuss "any issues relating to . . . electronically stored information, including the form or forms in which it should be produced." Consistent changes are made in other proposed amendments addressing the form of production as well.

Proposed new Rule 26(f)(4) adds issues relating to the assertion of privilege and work-product protection to the list of topics to be addressed in the parties' initial conference. For years, the Committee has wrestled with how to address the problem of privilege waivers within the rules. The Committee began this work in response to concerns over the expense and delay attendant to reviewing hard-copy documents for privilege and generating a privilege log. During the study of electronic discovery, the Committee learned that reviewing electronically stored information for privilege and work product protection adds to the expense and delay, and risk of waiver, because of the added volume, the dynamic nature of the information, and the complexities

Advisory Committee Report

of locating potentially privileged information. Metadata and embedded data are examples of such complexities; they may contain privileged communications, yet are not visible when the information is displayed on a computer monitor in ordinary use or printed on paper. Parties can ameliorate some of the costs and delays created by the steps necessary to avoid waiving privilege or work-product protection during discovery through agreements that allow the assertion of privilege or work production protection after documents or electronically stored information are produced. Including this topic among those to be discussed encourages early attention to the problem and facilitates efforts to reach such agreements. Form 35 is amended to provide that if the parties have agreed to an order regarding claims of privilege or protection as trial-preparation material asserted after production, they are to include a description of the proposed order provisions in their report to the court. Rule 16(b)(6) is amended to state that if the parties have reached an agreement for "asserting claims of privilege or protection as trial-preparation material after production," the court may include those agreements in the scheduling order.

The proposed rule as published described the topic that the parties should discuss as whether, if the parties agreed, the court should enter an order protecting the right to assert privilege after production. During the comment period, some expressed uneasiness about the language that the court enter an order "protecting" against waiver of privilege because it is not clear that this protection is effective against third parties. The Committee has revised the proposed rule and note language to meet these concerns, without changing the substance of what this aspect of the parties' discovery planning conference is to include.

Many comments urged the Committee to include work-product protection as well as privilege within this rule, as well as proposed Rule 26(b)(5)(B). Although the consequences of waiver are less acute for work product protection than for attorney-client privilege, many documents and electronically stored information involve both and issues of waiver frequently involve both. The Committee decided to amend the published proposed rule to include both privilege and work-product protection, using the label for such protection that appears elsewhere in the discovery rules, "trial-preparation materials."

The Proposed Rules and Committee Notes

The Advisory Committee recommends approval for adoption of amended Rules 16(b), 26(a), 26(f), and Form 35.

Rule 16(b)

The Committee recommends approval of the following amendment:

Rule 16. Pretrial Conferences; Scheduling; Management

* * * * *

(b) Scheduling and Planning. Except in categories of actions exempted by district court rule as inappropriate, the district judge, or a magistrate judge when authorized by district court rule, shall, after receiving the report from the parties under Rule 26(f) or after consulting with the attorneys for the parties and any unrepresented parties by a scheduling conference, telephone, mail, or other suitable means, enter a scheduling order that limits the time

(1) to join other parties and to amend the pleadings;

(2) to file motions; and

(3) to complete discovery.

The scheduling order also may include

(4) modifications of the times for disclosures under Rules 26(a) and 26(e)(1) and of the extent of discovery to be permitted;

<u>(5) provisions for disclosure or discovery of electronically stored information;</u>

<u>(6) any agreements the parties reach for asserting claims of privilege or of protection as trial-preparation material after production;</u>

(5)<u>(7)</u> the date or dates for conferences before trial, a final pretrial conference, and trial; and

(6)<u>(8)</u> any other matters appropriate in the circumstances of the case.

The order shall issue as soon as practicable but in any event within 90 days after the appearance of a defendant and within

120 days after the complaint has been served on a defendant. A schedule shall not be modified except upon a showing of good cause and by leave of the district judge or, when authorized by local rule, by a magistrate judge.

* * * * *

Committee Note

The amendment to Rule 16(b) is designed to alert the court to the possible need to address the handling of discovery of electronically stored information early in the litigation if such discovery is expected to occur. Rule 26(f) is amended to direct the parties to discuss discovery of electronically stored information if such discovery is contemplated in the action. Form 35 is amended to call for a report to the court about the results of this discussion. In many instances, the court's involvement early in the litigation will help avoid difficulties that might otherwise arise.

Rule 16(b) is also amended to include among the topics that may be addressed in the scheduling order any agreements that the parties reach to facilitate discovery by minimizing the risk of waiver of privilege or work-product protection. Rule 26(f) is amended to add to the discovery plan the parties' proposal for the court to enter a case-management or other order adopting such an agreement. The parties may agree to various arrangements. For example, they may agree to initial provision of requested materials without waiver of privilege or protection to enable the party seeking production to designate the materials desired or protection for actual production, with the privilege review of only those materials to follow. Alternatively, they may agree that if privileged or protected information is inadvertently produced, the producing party may by timely notice assert the privilege or protection and obtain return of the materials without waiver. Other arrangements are possible. In most circumstances, a party who receives information under such an arrangement cannot assert that production of the information waived a claim of privilege or of protection as trial-preparation material.

An order that includes the parties' agreement may be helpful in avoiding delay and excessive cost in discovery. See Manual for Complex Litigation (4th) § 11.446. Rule 16(b)(6) recognizes the propriety of including such agreements in the court's order. The rule does not provide the court with authority to enter such a case-management or other order without party agreement, or limit the court's authority to act on motion.

Changes Made After Publication and Comment

This recommendation is of a modified version of the proposal as published. Subdivision (b)(6) was modified to eliminate the references to "adopting" agreements for "protection against waiving" privilege. It was feared that these words might seem to promise greater protection than can be assured. In keeping with changes to Rule 26(b)(5)(B), subdivision (b)(6)

Rule 16(b)

was expanded to include agreements for asserting claims of protection as trial-preparation materials. The Committee Note was revised to reflect the changes in the rule text.

The proposed changes from the published rule are set out below.

Rule 16. Pretrial Conferences; Scheduling; Management*

* * * * *

(b) Scheduling and Planning.

* * * * *

The scheduling order may also include

* * * * *

(6) ~~adoption of the parties'~~ <u>any</u> agreements <u>the parties</u> <u>reach for</u> ~~protection against waiving~~ <u>asserting claims of</u> privilege <u>or of protection as trial-preparation material after</u> <u>production</u>;

* * * * *

Rule 26(a)

The Committee recommends approval of the following amendment:

Rule 26. General Provisions Governing Discovery; Duty of Disclosure

(a) Required Disclosures; Methods to Discover Additional Matter.

(1) **Initial Disclosures.** Except in categories of proceedings specified in Rule 26(a)(1)(E), or to the extent otherwise stipulated or directed by order, a party must, without awaiting a discovery request, provide to other parties:

(A) the name and, if known, the address and telephone

*Changes from the proposal published for public comment shown by double-underlining new material and striking through omitted matter.

number of each individual likely to have discoverable information that the disclosing party may use to support its claims or defenses, unless solely for impeachment, identifying the subjects of the information;

(B) a copy of, or a description by category and location of, all documents, <u>electronically stored information,</u> ~~data compilations,~~ and tangible things that are in the possession, custody, or control of the party and that the disclosing party may use to support its claims or defenses, unless solely for impeachment;

* * * * *

Committee Note

Subdivision (a). Rule 26(a)(1)(B) is amended to parallel Rule 34(a) by recognizing that a party must disclose electronically stored information as well as documents that it may use to support its claims or defenses. The term "electronically stored information" has the same broad meaning in Rule 26(a)(1) as in Rule 34(a). This amendment is consistent with the 1993 addition of Rule 26(a)(1)(B). The term "data compilations" is deleted as unnecessary because it is a subset of both documents and electronically stored information.

Changes Made After Publication and Comment

As noted in the introduction, this provision was not included in the published rule. It is included as a conforming amendment, to make Rule 26(a)(1) consistent with the changes that were included in the published proposals.

Rule 26(f)

The Committee recommends approval of the following amendments to Rule 26(f).

Rule 26. General Provisions Governing Discovery; Duty of Disclosure

* * * * *

(f) Conference of Parties; Planning for Discovery. Except in categories of proceedings exempted from initial disclosure under Rule 26(a)(1)(E) or when otherwise ordered, the parties must, as soon as practicable and in any event at least 21 days before a scheduling conference is held or a scheduling order is due under Rule 16(b), confer to consider the nature and basis of their claims and defenses and the possibilities for a prompt settlement or resolution of the case, to make or arrange for the disclosures required by Rule 26(a)(1), <u>to discuss any issues relating to preserving discoverable information,</u> and to develop a proposed discovery plan that indicates the parties' views and proposals concerning:

(1) what changes should be made in the timing, form, or requirement for disclosures under Rule 26(a), including a statement as to when disclosures under Rule 26(a)(1) were made or will be made;

(2) the subjects on which discovery may be needed, when discovery should be completed, and whether discovery should be conducted in phases or be limited to or focused upon particular issues;

<u>(3)</u> <u>any issues relating to disclosure or discovery of electronically stored information, including the form or forms in which it should be produced;</u>

<u>(4)</u> <u>any issues relating to claims of privilege or of protection as trial-preparation material, including — if the parties agree on a procedure to assert such claims after production — whether to ask the court to include their agreement in an order;</u>

~~(3)~~<u>(5)</u> what changes should be made in the limitations on discovery imposed under these rules or by local rule, and what other limitations should be imposed; and

~~(4)~~**(6)** any other orders that should be entered by the court under Rule 26(c) or under Rule 16(b) and (c).

* * * * *

Committee Note

Subdivision (f). Rule 26(f) is amended to direct the parties to discuss discovery of electronically stored information during their discovery-planning conference. The rule focuses on "issues relating to disclosure or discovery of electronically stored information"; the discussion is not required in cases not involving electronic discovery, and the amendment imposes no additional requirements in those cases. When the parties do anticipate disclosure or discovery of electronically stored information, discussion at the outset may avoid later difficulties or ease their resolution.

When a case involves discovery of electronically stored information, the issues to be addressed during the Rule 26(f) conference depend on the nature and extent of the contemplated discovery and of the parties' information systems. It may be important for the parties to discuss those systems, and accordingly important for counsel to become familiar with those systems before the conference. With that information, the parties can develop a discovery plan that takes into account the capabilities of their computer systems. In appropriate cases identification of, and early discovery from, individuals with special knowledge of a party's computer systems may be helpful.

The particular issues regarding electronically stored information that deserve attention during the discovery planning stage depend on the specifics of the given case. See Manual for Complex Litigation (4th) § 40.25(2) (listing topics for discussion in a proposed order regarding meet-and-confer sessions). For example, the parties may specify the topics for such discovery and the time period for which discovery will be sought. They may identify the various sources of such information within a party's control that should be searched for electronically stored information. They may discuss whether the information is reasonably accessible to the party that has it, including the burden or cost of retrieving and reviewing the information. See Rule 26(b)(2)(B). Rule 26(f)(3) explicitly directs the parties to discuss the form or forms in which electronically stored information might be produced. The parties may be able to reach agreement on the forms of production, making discovery more efficient. Rule 34(b) is amended to permit a requesting party to specify the form or forms in which it wants electronically stored information produced. If the requesting party does not specify a form, Rule 34(b) directs the responding party to state the forms it intends to use in the production. Early discussion of the forms of production may facilitate the application of Rule 34(b) by allowing the parties to determine what forms of production will meet both parties' needs. Early identification of disputes over the forms of production may help avoid the expense and delay of searches or productions using inappropriate forms.

Rule 26(f) is also amended to direct the parties to discuss any issues regarding preservation of discoverable information during their conference

Rule 26(f)

as they develop a discovery plan. This provision applies to all sorts of discoverable information, but can be particularly important with regard to electronically stored information. The volume and dynamic nature of electronically stored information may complicate preservation obligations. The ordinary operation of computers involves both the automatic creation and the automatic deletion or overwriting of certain information. Failure to address preservation issues early in the litigation increases uncertainty and raises a risk of disputes.

The parties' discussion should pay particular attention to the balance between the competing needs to preserve relevant evidence and to continue routine operations critical to ongoing activities. Complete or broad cessation of a party's routine computer operations could paralyze the party's activities. Cf. Manual for Complex Litigation (4th) § 11.422 ("A blanket preservation order may be prohibitively expensive and unduly burdensome for parties dependent on computer systems for their day-to-day operations.") The parties should take account of these considerations in their discussions, with the goal of agreeing on reasonable preservation steps.

The requirement that the parties discuss preservation does not imply that courts should routinely enter preservation orders. A preservation order entered over objections should be narrowly tailored. Ex parte preservation orders should issue only in exceptional circumstances.

Rule 26(f) is also amended to provide that the parties should discuss any issues relating to assertions of privilege or of protection as trial-preparation materials, including whether the parties can facilitate discovery by agreeing on procedures for asserting claims of privilege or protection after production and whether to ask the court to enter an order that includes any agreement the parties reach. The Committee has repeatedly been advised about the discovery difficulties that can result from efforts to guard against waiver of privilege and work-product protection. Frequently parties find it necessary to spend large amounts of time reviewing materials requested through discovery to avoid waiving privilege. These efforts are necessary because materials subject to a claim of privilege or protection are often difficult to identify. A failure to withhold even one such item may result in an argument that there has been a waiver of privilege as to all other privileged materials on that subject matter. Efforts to avoid the risk of waiver can impose substantial costs on the party producing the material and the time required for the privilege review can substantially delay access for the party seeking discovery.

These problems often become more acute when discovery of electronically stored information is sought. The volume of such data, and the informality that attends use of e-mail and some other types of electronically stored information, may make privilege determinations more difficult, and privilege review correspondingly more expensive and time consuming. Other aspects of electronically stored information pose particular difficulties for privilege review. For example, production may be sought of information automatically included in electronic files but not apparent to the creator or to readers. Computer programs may retain draft language, editorial comments, and other deleted matter (sometimes referred to as "embedded data" or "embedded edits") in an electronic file but not make them apparent to the reader. Information describing the history, tracking, or management of an electronic file (sometimes called "metadata") is usually not apparent to the reader viewing a hard copy or a screen image. Whether this information should be produced may be among the topics discussed in the Rule 26(f) conference. If it is, it may need to be reviewed to ensure that no privileged information is included, further complicating the task of privilege review.

Parties may attempt to minimize these costs and delays by agreeing to protocols that minimize the risk of waiver. They may agree that the responding party will provide certain requested materials for initial examination without waiving any privilege or protection — sometimes known as a "quick peek." The requesting party then designates the documents it wishes to have actually produced. This designation is the Rule 34 request. The responding party then responds in the usual course, screening only those documents actually requested for formal production and asserting privilege claims as provided in Rule 26(b)(5)(A). On other occasions, parties enter agreements — sometimes called "clawback agreements"— that production without intent to waive privilege or protection should not be a waiver so long as the responding party identifies the documents mistakenly produced, and that the documents should be returned under those circumstances. Other voluntary arrangements may be appropriate depending on the circumstances of each litigation. In most circumstances, a party who receives information under such an arrangement cannot assert that production of the information waived a claim of privilege or of protection as trial-preparation material.

Although these agreements may not be appropriate for all cases, in certain cases they can facilitate prompt and economical discovery by reducing delay before the discovering party obtains access to documents, and by reducing the cost and burden of review by the producing party. A case-management or other order including such agreements may further facilitate the discovery process. Form 35 is amended to include a report to the court about any agreement regarding protections against inadvertent forfeiture or waiver of privilege or protection that the parties have reached, and Rule 16(b) is amended to recognize that the court may include such an agreement in a case-management or other order. If the parties agree to entry of such an order, their proposal should be included in the report to the court.

Rule 26(b)(5)(B) is added to establish a parallel procedure to assert privilege or protection as trial-preparation material after production, leaving the question of waiver to later determination by the court.

Changes Made After Publication and Comment

The Committee recommends a modified version of what was published. Rule 26(f)(3) was expanded to refer to the form "or forms" of production, in parallel with the like change in Rule 34. Different forms may be suitable for different sources of electronically stored information.

The published Rule 26(f)(4) proposal described the parties' views and proposals concerning whether, on their agreement, the court should enter

Rule 26(f)

an order protecting the right to assert privilege after production. This has been revised to refer to the parties' views and proposals concerning any issues relating to claims of privilege, including — if the parties agree on a procedure to assert such claims after production — whether to ask the court to include their agreement in an order. As with Rule 16(b)(6), this change was made to avoid any implications as to the scope of the protection that may be afforded by court adoption of the parties' agreement.

Rule 26(f)(4) also was expanded to include trial-preparation materials.

The Committee Note was revised to reflect the changes in the rule text.

The changes from the published rule are shown below.

Rule 26. General Provisions Governing Discovery; Duty of Disclosure*

* * * * *

(f) Conference of Parties; Planning for Discovery. Except   in categories of proceedings exempted from initial disclosure under Rule 26(a)(1)(E) or when otherwise ordered, the parties must, as soon as practicable and in any event at least 21 days before a scheduling conference is held or a scheduling order is due under Rule 16(b), confer to consider the nature and basis of their claims and defenses and the possibilities for a prompt settlement or resolution of the case, to make or arrange for the disclosures required by Rule 26(a)(1), to discuss any issues relating to preserving discoverable information, and to develop a proposed discovery plan that indicates the parties' views and proposals concerning:

* * * * *

(3) any issues relating to disclosure or discovery of electronically stored information, including the form <u>or forms</u> in which it should be produced;

(4) <u>any issues relating to claims of privilege or protec-</u>

---

*Changes from the proposal published for public comment shown by double-underlining new material and striking through omitted matter.

tion as trial-preparation material, including – if the parties
agree on a procedure to assert such claims after production
– whether to ask the court to include their agreement in
an order; ~~whether, on agreement of the parties, the court
should enter an order protecting the right to assert privilege
after production of privileged information;~~

* * * * *

Form 35

The Committee recommends conforming changes in Form 35, the parties' report to the court of their discovery plan.

Form 35. Report of Parties' Planning Meeting

* * * * *

3. Discovery Plan. The parties jointly propose to the court the following discovery plan: [Use separate paragraphs or subparagraphs as necessary if parties disagree.]

Discovery will be needed on the following subjects:
_____ (brief description of subjects on which discovery will be needed)_____

Disclosure or discovery of electronically stored information should be handled as follows: _____ (brief description of parties' proposals)_____

The parties have agreed to an order regarding claims of privilege or of protection as trial-preparation material asserted after production, as follows: (brief description of provisions of proposed order)

All discovery commenced in time to be completed by _____(date)_____. [Discovery on _____(issue for early discovery)_____to be completed by _____ (date)_____.]

Form 35

Changes Made After Publication and Comment

The Committee recommends approval of Form 35 with modifications made from the published version, consistent with changes made to Rule 26(f). The changes are shown below.

Form 35. Report of Parties' Planning Meeting*

* * * * *

3. Discovery Plan. The parties jointly propose to the court the following discovery plan: * * *

Disclosure or discovery of electronically stored information should be handled as follows: _____(brief description of parties' proposals)

The parties have agreed to ~~a privilege protection~~ an order <u>regarding claims of privilege or of protection as trial-preparation material asserted after production,</u> as follows: (brief description of provisions of proposed order). * * *

* * * * *

ii. Discovery Into Electronically Stored Information that is Not Reasonably Accessible: Rule 26(b)(2)

Introduction

The Rule 26(b)(2)(B) proposal authorizes a party to respond to a discovery request by identifying sources of electronically stored information that are not reasonably accessible because of undue burden or cost. If the requesting party seeks discovery from such sources, the responding party has the burden to show that the sources are not reasonably accessible. Even if that showing is made, the court may order discovery if — after considering the limitations established by present Rule 26(b)(2) — the requesting party shows good cause. The court may specify conditions for the discovery.

Several changes have been made in the rule text to express more clearly the procedure established by the published proposal. The Committee Note is revised to describe more clearly the problems that the rule addresses. The changes both in rule text and Note draw from a large body of public testimony and comments that suggested better ways to implement the proposed

---

*Changes from the proposal published for public comment shown by double underlining new material and striking through omitted matter.

procedure without changing the procedure established by the published language.

The proposed rule has frequently been referred to as a "two-tier" system. It responds to distinctive problems encountered in discovery of electronically stored information that have no close analogue in the more familiar discovery of paper documents. Although computer storage often facilitates discovery, some forms of computer storage can be searched only with considerable effort. The responding party may be able to identify difficult-to-access sources that may contain responsive information, but is not able to retrieve the information — or even to determine whether any responsive information in fact is on the sources — without incurring substantial burden or cost. The difficulties in accessing the information may arise from a number of different reasons primarily related to the technology of information storage, reasons that are likely to change over time. Examples from current technology include back-up tapes intended for disaster recovery purposes that are often not indexed, organized, or susceptible to electronic searching; legacy data that remains from obsolete systems and is unintelligible on the successor systems; data that was "deleted" but remains in fragmented form, requiring a modern version of forensics to restore and retrieve; and databases that were designed to create certain information in certain ways and that cannot readily create very different kinds or forms of information. Such difficulties present particular problems for discovery. A party may have a large amount of information on sources or in forms that may be responsive to discovery requests, but would require recovery, restoration, or translation before it could be located, retrieved, reviewed, or produced. At the same time, more easily accessed sources — whether computer-based, paper, or human — may yield all the information that is reasonably useful for the action. Lawyers sophisticated in these problems are developing a two-tier practice in which they first sort through the information that can be provided from easily accessed sources and then determine whether it is necessary to search the difficult-to-access sources.

In many circumstances, the two-tier approach will be worked out by negotiation. The Rule 26(b)(2)(B) amendment expressly incorporates the better practice as the method for judicial control when the parties cannot resolve the problem on their own. The amendment builds on the two-tier structure of scope of discovery defined in Rule 26(b)(1) and applies this structure to discovery of electronically stored information. The proposed rule recognizes a distinctive, recurring problem that electronically stored information presents for discovery and builds on the existing rules to facilitate judicial supervision when it is necessary to calibrate discovery to a particular case.

Much of the criticism during the public comment period focused on specific drafting problems in the published rule, including a lack of clarity

Rule 26(b)(2)

in the term "not reasonably accessible," how that term and the "good cause" showing related to the existing Rule 26(b)(2) proportionality limits, and how a party designation or a court finding that information is not reasonably accessible related to preservation obligations. The proposed rule and Note have been revised to respond to the concerns identified.

The published rule required a party to identify potentially responsive "information" that is not reasonably accessible. The problem, however, is that a responding party cannot identify information without actually searching and retrieving it. The revised rule directs the party to identify the sources of information that may be responsive but is not reasonably accessible.

The published rule did not provide any guide to the considerations that bear on determining whether electronically stored information is not reasonably accessible. Many comments suggested that the test should be based on the burden and cost of locating, restoring, and retrieving potentially responsive information from the sources in which it is stored. The revised rule incorporates this test, which reflects the common understanding of the published proposal. The responding party may identify sources containing potentially responsive information that is not reasonably accessible "because of undue burden or cost."

Once the responding party has identified a source of information that is not reasonably accessible, the published rule provided for a motion to compel discovery. The revision recognizes that the responding party may wish to resolve the issue by moving for a protective order. Among the reasons that may lead a responding party to raise the issue is to resolve whether, or the extent to which, it must preserve the information stored on the difficult-to-access sources until discoverability is resolved.

A finding that the responding party has shown that a source of information is not reasonably accessible does not preclude discovery; the court may order discovery for good cause. Many comments suggested that the "good cause" standard seemed to contemplate the limitations identified by parts (i), (ii), and (iii) of present Rule 26(b)(2). The revised text clarifies the "good cause" showing by expressly referring to consideration of these limitations.

The Committee Note is revised extensively to provide a clearer description of the two-tier procedure. It recognizes that in some cases a single proceeding may suffice both to find that a source is not reasonably accessible and also to determine whether good cause nonetheless justifies discovery and to set any conditions that should be imposed. But it also recognizes that proceedings may need to be staged if focused discovery is necessary to determine the costs and burdens in obtaining the information from the sources identified as not reasonably accessible, the likelihood of finding responsive information on such sources, and the value of the information to the litigation. In such circumstances, a finding that a source is not reasonably accessible may lead to further proceedings to determine whether there is good cause to order limited or extensive searches and the production of information stored on such sources.

The proposed amendment is modest. The public comments and testimony confirmed that parties conducting discovery, particularly when it involves large volumes of information, first look in the places that are likely to produce responsive information. Parties sophisticated in electronic discovery first look in the reasonably accessible places that are likely to produce responsive information. On that level, stating in the rule that initial production of information that is not reasonably accessible is not required simply recognizes reality. Under proposed Rule 26(b)(2), this existing practice would continue; parties would search sources that are reasonably accessible and likely to contain responsive, relevant information, with no need for a court order. But in an improvement over the present practice, in which parties simply do not produce inaccessible electronically stored information, the amendment requires the responding party to identify the sources of information that were not searched, clarifying and focusing the issue for the requesting party. In many cases, discovery obtained from accessible sources will be sufficient to meet the needs of the case. If information from such sources does not satisfy the requesting party, the proposed rule allows that party to obtain additional discovery from sources identified as not reasonably accessible, subject to judicial supervision.

One criticism leveled against the proposal is that it allows the responding party to "self-designate" information not produced because it is not reasonably accessible. All party-managed discovery and privilege invocation rests on "self-designation" to some extent. That is happening now, without the insights for the requesting party that the identification requirement provides. The responding party must disclose categories and types of sources of potentially responsive information that are not searched, enabling the requesting party to decide whether to challenge that designation.

Two other areas of concern were expressed during the comment period. One is the relationship to preservation. A second, related concern is that this proposal would lead corporations to make information inaccessible in order to frustrate discovery. As to the first concern, the Note is revised to clarify that the rule does not undermine or reduce common-law or statutory preservation obligations. The Committee Note includes a reminder that a party may be obliged to preserve information stored on sources it has identified as not reasonably accessible, but in keeping with the approach taken in proposed Rule 37(f) does not attempt to state or define a preservation obligation. As to the second concern, many witnesses and comments rejected the argument that

Rule 26(b)(2)

the rule would encourage entities or individuals to "bury" information that is necessary or useful for business purposes or that regulations or statutes require them to retain. Moreover, the rule requires that the information identified as not reasonably accessible must be difficult to access by the producing party for all purposes, not for a particular litigation. A party that makes information "inaccessible" because it is likely to be discoverable in litigation is subject to sanctions now and would still be subject to sanctions under the proposed rule changes.

The Proposed Rule and Committee Note

Rule 26(b)(2)

The Committee recommends approval of the following amendment:

Rule 26. General Provisions Governing Discovery; Duty of Disclosure

* * * * *

(b) Discovery Scope and Limits. Unless otherwise limited by order of the court in accordance with these rules, the scope of discovery is as follows:

* * * * *

(2) Limitations.

<u>**(A)**</u> By order, the court may alter the limits in these rules on the number of depositions and interrogatories or the length of depositions under Rule 30. By order or local rule, the court may also limit the number of requests under Rule 36.

<u>**(B)** A party need not provide discovery of electronically stored information from sources that the party identifies as not reasonably accessible because of undue burden or cost. On motion to compel discovery or for a protective order, the party from whom discovery is sought must show that the information is not reasonably accessible because of undue bur-</u>

den or cost. If that showing is made, the court may
nonetheless order discovery from such sources if
the requesting party shows good cause, considering
the limitations of Rule 26(b)(2)(C). The court may
specify conditions for the discovery.

(C) The frequency or extent of use of the discovery methods otherwise permitted under these
rules and by any local rule shall be limited by the
court if it determines that: (i) the discovery sought
is unreasonably cumulative or duplicative, or is ob-
tainable from some other source that is more convenient, less burdensome, or less expensive; (ii) the
party seeking discovery has had ample opportunity
by discovery in the action to obtain the information
sought; or (iii) the burden or expense of the proposed discovery outweighs its likely benefit, taking
into account the needs of the case, the amount in
controversy, the parties' resources, the importance
of the issues at stake in the litigation, and the importance of the proposed discovery in resolving the
issues. The court may act upon its own initiative
after reasonable notice or pursuant to a motion under Rule 26(c).

* * * * *

Committee Note

Subdivision (b)(2). The amendment to Rule 26(b)(2) is designed to
address issues raised by difficulties in locating, retrieving, and providing
discovery of some electronically stored information. Electronic storage
systems often make it easier to locate and retrieve information. These
advantages are properly taken into account in determining the reasonable
scope of discovery in a particular case. But some sources of electronically

stored information can be accessed only with substantial burden and cost. In a particular case, these burdens and costs may make the information on such sources not reasonably accessible.

It is not possible to define in a rule the different types of technological features that may affect the burdens and costs of accessing electronically stored information. Information systems are designed to provide ready access to information used in regular ongoing activities. They also may be designed so as to provide ready access to information that is not regularly used. But a system may retain information on sources that are accessible only by incurring substantial burdens or costs. Subparagraph (B) is added to regulate discovery from such sources.

Under this rule, a responding party should produce electronically stored information that is relevant, not privileged, and reasonably accessible, subject to the (b)(2)(C) limitations that apply to all discovery. The responding party must also identify, by category or type, the sources containing potentially responsive information that it is neither searching nor producing. The identification should, to the extent possible, provide enough detail to enable the requesting party to evaluate the burdens and costs of providing the discovery and the likelihood of finding responsive information on the identified sources.

A party's identification of sources of electronically stored information as not reasonably accessible does not relieve the party of its common-law or statutory duties to preserve evidence. Whether a responding party is required to preserve unsearched sources of potentially responsive information that it believes are not reasonably accessible depends on the circumstances of each case. It is often useful for the parties to discuss this issue early in discovery.

The volume of — and the ability to search — much electronically stored information means that in many cases the responding party will be able to produce information from reasonably accessible sources that will fully satisfy the parties' discovery needs. In many circumstances the requesting party should obtain and evaluate the information from such sources before insisting that the responding party search and produce information contained on sources that are not reasonably accessible. If the requesting party continues to seek discovery of information from sources identified as not reasonably accessible, the parties should discuss the burdens and costs of accessing and retrieving the information, the needs that may establish good cause for requiring all or part of the requested discovery even if the information sought is not reasonably accessible, and conditions on obtaining and producing the information that may be appropriate.

If the parties cannot agree whether, or on what terms, sources identified as not reasonably accessible should be searched and discoverable information produced, the issue may be raised either by a motion to compel discovery or by a motion for a protective order. The parties must confer before bringing either motion. If the parties do not resolve the issue and the court must decide, the responding party must show that the identified sources of information are not reasonably accessible because of undue burden or cost. The requesting party may need discovery to test this assertion. Such discovery might take the form of requiring the responding party to conduct a sampling of information contained on the sources identified as not reasonably accessible; allowing some form of inspection of such sources; or taking depositions of witnesses knowledgeable about the responding party's information systems.

Once it is shown that a source of electronically stored information is not reasonably accessible, the requesting party may still obtain discovery by showing good cause, considering the limitations of Rule 26(b)(2)(C) that balance the costs and potential benefits of discovery. The decision whether to require a responding party to search for and produce information that is not reasonably accessible depends not only on the burdens and costs of doing so, but also on whether those burdens and costs can be justified in the circumstances of the case. Appropriate considerations may include: (1) the specificity of the discovery request; (2) the quantity of information available from other and more easily accessed sources; (3) the failure to produce relevant information that seems likely to have existed but is no longer available on more easily accessed sources; (4) the likelihood of finding relevant, responsive information that cannot be obtained from other, more easily accessed sources; (5) predictions as to the importance and usefulness of the further information; (6) the importance of the issues at stake in the litigation; and (7) the parties' resources.

The responding party has the burden as to one aspect of the inquiry — whether the identified sources are not reasonably accessible in light of the burdens and costs required to search for, retrieve, and produce whatever responsive information may be found. The requesting party has the burden of showing that its need for the discovery outweighs the burdens and costs of locating, retrieving, and producing the information. In some cases, the court will be able to determine whether the identified sources are not reasonably accessible and whether the requesting party has shown good cause for some or all of the discovery, consistent with the limitations of Rule 26(b)(2)(C), through a single proceeding or presentation. The good-cause determination, however, may be complicated because the court and parties may know little about what information the sources identified as not reasonably accessible might contain, whether it is relevant, or how valuable it may be to the litigation. In such cases, the parties may need some focused discovery, which may include sampling of the sources, to learn more about what burdens and costs are involved in accessing the information, what the information consists of, and how valuable it is for the litigation in light of information that can be obtained by exhausting other opportunities for discovery.

The good-cause inquiry and consideration of the Rule 26(b)(2)(C) limitations are coupled with the authority to set conditions for discovery. The conditions may take the form of limits on the amount, type, or sources of information required to be accessed and produced. The conditions may also include payment by the requesting party of part or all of the reasonable costs of obtaining information from sources that are not reasonably accessible. A requesting party's willingness to share or bear the access costs may be weighed by the court in determining whether there is good cause. But

Rule 26(b)(2)

the producing party's burdens in reviewing the information for relevance and privilege may weigh against permitting the requested discovery.

The limitations of Rule 26(b)(2)(C) continue to apply to all discovery of electronically stored information, including that stored on reasonably accessible electronic sources.

Changes Made after Publication and Comment

This recommendation modifies the version of the proposed rule amendment as published. Responding to comments that the published proposal seemed to require identification of information that cannot be identified because it is not reasonably accessible, the rule text was clarified by requiring identification of sources that are not reasonably accessible. The test of reasonable accessibility was clarified by adding "because of undue burden or cost."

The published proposal referred only to a motion by the requesting party to compel discovery. The rule text has been changed to recognize that the responding party may wish to determine its search and potential preservation obligations by moving for a protective order.

The provision that the court may for good cause order discovery from sources that are not reasonably accessible is expanded in two ways. It now states specifically that the requesting party is the one who must show good cause, and it refers to consideration of the limitations on discovery set out in present Rule 26(b)(2)(i), (ii), and (iii).

The published proposal was added at the end of present Rule 26(b)(2). It has been relocated to become a new subparagraph (B), allocating present Rule 26(b)(2) to new subparagraphs (A) and (C). The Committee Note was changed to reflect the rule text revisions. It also was shortened. The shortening was accomplished in part by deleting references to problems that are likely to become antique as technology continues to evolve, and in part by deleting passages that were at a level of detail better suited for a practice manual than a Committee Note.

The changes from the published proposed amendment to Rule 26(b)(2) are set out below.

Rule 26. General Provisions Governing Discovery; Duty of Disclosure*

(b) Discovery Scope and Limits. Unless otherwise limited by order of the court in accordance with these rules, the scope of discovery is as follows:

* * * * *

---

*Changes from the proposal published for public comment shown by double-underlining new material and striking through omitted matter.

(2) Limitations.

* * * * *

(B) A party need not provide discovery of electronically stored information <u>from sources</u> that the party identifies as not reasonably accessible <u>because of undue burden or cost</u>. On motion ~~by the requesting party~~ <u>to compel discovery or for a protective order</u>, the ~~responding~~ party <u>from whom discovery is sought</u> must show that the information is not reasonably accessible <u>because of undue burden or cost</u>. If that showing is made, the court may <u>nonetheless</u> order discovery ~~of the information~~ <u>from such sources</u> ~~for~~ <u>if the requesting party shows</u> good cause<u>, considering the limitations of Rule 26(b)(2)(C).</u>~~and~~ The court may specify ~~terms and~~ conditions for the discovery.

(C) . . . . ~~A party need not provide discovery of electronically stored information that the party identifies as not reasonably accessible. On motion by the requesting party, the responding party must show that the information is not reasonably accessible. If that showing is made, the court may order discovery of the information for good cause and may specify terms and conditions for such discovery.~~

Rule 26(b)(5)

iii. Procedure For Asserting Claims of Privilege and Work Product Protection After Production: Rule 26(b)(5)

Introduction

Ever since the Committee began its intensive examination of discovery in 1996, a frequent complaint has been the expense and delay that accompany privilege review. The Committee has long studied whether it could offer a rule that would helpfully address this problem, within the limitations of the Rules Enabling Act and 28 U.S.C. § 2074(b). The Committee's more recent focus on electronic discovery revealed that the problems of privilege review are often more acute in that setting than with conventional discovery. The volume of electronically stored information responsive to discovery and the varying ways such information is stored and displayed make it more difficult to review for privilege than paper. The production of privileged material is a substantial risk and the costs and delay caused by privilege review are increasingly problematic. The proposed amendment to Rule 26(b)(5) addresses these problems by setting up a procedure to assert privilege and work-product protection claims after production.

Under the proposed rule, if a party has produced information in discovery that it claims is privileged or protected as trial-preparation material, that party may notify the receiving party of the claim, stating the basis for it. After receiving notification, the receiving party must return, sequester, or destroy the information, and may not use or disclose it to third parties until the claim is resolved. The receiving party has the option of submitting the information directly to the court to decide whether the information is privileged or protected as claimed and, if so, whether a waiver has occurred. A receiving party that has disclosed or provided the information to a nonparty before getting notice must take reasonable steps to obtain the return of the information. The producing party must preserve the information pending the court's ruling on whether the information is privileged or protected and whether any privilege or work product protection has been waived or forfeited by production.

The proposed amendment does not address the substantive questions whether privilege or work product protection has been waived or forfeited. Instead, the amendment sets up a procedure to allow the responding party to assert a claim of privilege or of work-product protection after production. This supplements the existing procedure in Rule 26(b)(5) for a party that has withheld information on the ground of privilege or of protection to assert the claim, the requesting party to contest the claim, and the court to resolve the dispute. It is a nod to the pressures of litigating with the amount and nature of electronically stored information available in the present age, a procedural device for addressing the increasingly costly and time-consuming efforts to reduce the number of inevitable blunders.

The published rule addressed claims of privilege, but did not specifically include claims of protection as trial-preparation material. During the comment period, many suggested adding work- product protection to the rule. Doing so is consistent with present Rule 26(b)(5)(A) and reflects the reality that privilege and work- product protection often overlap; review is conducted simultaneously; and both have waiver consequences, although the extent may differ. The Committee decided to include both privilege and protection as trial-preparation material in the rule.

The published rule required the producing party to assert the claim of privilege within a "reasonable time." Several concerns were raised about the "reasonable time" provision that convinced the Committee to delete it from the proposed rule. Under the law of many jurisdictions, whether a party asserted a privilege claim within a reasonable time is important to determining whether there is a waiver; focusing on a reasonable time might carry implications inconsistent with the Committee's intent to avoid the substantive law of privilege and privilege waiver. In addition, the "reasonable time" formulation was not tied to any particular triggering event, such as the date of production or the date when the responding party learned or should have learned that it had produced information subject to a privilege or protection claim. A "reasonable time" requirement unmoored to a particular triggering event proved confusing. It is deleted from the revised proposal. The deletion does not mean that parties are free to assert a privilege or protection claim at any point in the litigation. Courts will continue to examine whether such a claim was made at a reasonable time, but as part of determining whether a waiver has occurred under the substantive law governing that issue.

The proposed rule is also revised to include what many comments recommended: a provision authorizing the receiving party to submit the information asserted to be privileged or protected under seal to the court. As a related change, the rule language is revised to require the party asserting the claim to set out the basis for it when giving notice; the Committee Note states that the receiving party should submit that statement to the court, along with the information itself, if the receiving party chooses to contest the claim. The notice informs the court of the basis for the claim and allows the receiving party to use the submission to seek a ruling as to waiver, privilege or protection, or both. Additional rule and Note language are provided to clarify this point.

As published, the Note stated that after receiving notice that information is claimed to be privileged, the party that received the information may not disseminate or use the information until the claim is resolved. Many comments urged that this directive be elevated to the rule. The Committee decided to add the directive to the rule text itself, adding clarity and emphasizing the purpose of providing a consistent and predictable procedure and preserving the status quo pending resolution of claims asserted after production.

Rule 26(b)(5)

The published rule did not specifically address an obligation by the receiving party to retrieve information it disclosed to third parties before the responding party asserted a privilege claim. Although the Committee Note stated that a receiving party should attempt to obtain return of the information if it had been disclosed to a nonparty, the absence of such language emerged as a concern during the comment period. The Committee decided to address this issue in the rule text, but to limit any such obligation to "reasonable steps" to retrieve such information. Such a formulation provides appropriate protection for the party asserting the claim pending its resolution, but also limits the burden on the receiving party.

The Committee specifically sought reaction during the comment period on whether to require the party that received the notice to certify compliance with the rule. There was little support for this addition during the comment period. One concern was that by requiring the creation of a new, separate document, such a provision would go beyond the certification that Rule 26(g) reads into the signature on a discovery document. Imposing an added requirement on a party that did not make the mistake precipitating the problem in the first place also raised concerns. The Committee decided not to include a certification requirement in the rule.

The Proposed Rule and Committee Note

Rule 26(b)(5)(B)

The Committee recommends approval of the following proposed amendment.

Rule 26. General Provisions Governing Discovery; Duty of Disclosure

* * * * *

(b) **Discovery Scope and Limits.** Unless otherwise limited by order of the court in accordance with these rules, the scope of discovery is as follows:

* * * * *

(5) **Claims of Privilege or Protection of Trial Preparation Materials.**

(A) **Information Withheld.** When a party withholds information otherwise discoverable under these rules by claiming that it is privileged or subject to protection as trial-preparation material, the party shall make the claim expressly and shall describe the nature of the documents, communications, or things not produced or disclosed in a manner that, without revealing information itself privileged or protected, will enable other parties to assess the applicability of the privilege or protection.

(B) Information Produced. If information is produced in discovery that is subject to a claim of privilege or of protection as trial-preparation material, the party making the claim may notify any party that received the information of the claim and the basis for it. After being notified, a party must promptly return, sequester, or destroy the specified information and any copies it has and may not use or disclose the information until the claim is resolved. A receiving party may promptly present the information to the court under seal for a determination of the claim. If the receiving party disclosed the information before being notified, it must take reasonable steps to retrieve it. The producing party must preserve the information until the claim is resolved.

* * * * *

Committee Note

Subdivision (b)(5). The Committee has repeatedly been advised that the risk of privilege waiver, and the work necessary to avoid it, add to the costs and delay of discovery. When the review is of electronically stored information, the risk of waiver, and the time and effort required to avoid it, can increase substantially because of the volume of electronically stored information and the difficulty in ensuring that all information to be produced

Rule 26(b)(5)

has in fact been reviewed. Rule 26(b)(5)(A) provides a procedure for a party that has withheld information on the basis of privilege or protection as trial-preparation material to make the claim so that the requesting party can decide whether to contest the claim and the court can resolve the dispute. Rule 26(b)(5)(B) is added to provide a procedure for a party to assert a claim of privilege or trial-preparation material protection after information is produced in discovery in the action and, if the claim is contested, permit any party that received the information to present the matter to the court for resolution.

Rule 26(b)(5)(B) does not address whether the privilege or protection that is asserted after production was waived by the production. The courts have developed principles to determine whether, and under what circumstances, waiver results from inadvertent production of privileged or protected information. Rule 26(b)(5)(B) provides a procedure for presenting and addressing these issues. Rule 26(b)(5)(B) works in tandem with Rule 26(f), which is amended to direct the parties to discuss privilege issues in preparing their discovery plan, and which, with amended Rule 16(b), allows the parties to ask the court to include in an order any agreements the parties reach regarding issues of privilege or trial-preparation material protection. Agreements reached under Rule 26(f)(4) and orders including such agreements entered under Rule 16(b)(6) may be considered when a court determines whether a waiver has occurred. Such agreements and orders ordinarily control if they adopt procedures different from those in Rule 26(b)(5)(B).

A party asserting a claim of privilege or protection after production must give notice to the receiving party. That notice should be in writing unless the circumstances preclude it. Such circumstances could include the assertion of the claim during a deposition. The notice should be as specific as possible in identifying the information and stating the basis for the claim. Because the receiving party must decide whether to challenge the claim and may sequester the information and submit it to the court for a ruling on whether the claimed privilege or protection applies and whether it has been waived, the notice should be sufficiently detailed so as to enable the receiving party and the court to understand the basis for the claim and to determine whether waiver has occurred. Courts will continue to examine whether a claim of privilege or protection was made at a reasonable time when delay is part of the waiver determination under the governing law.

After receiving notice, each party that received the information must promptly return, sequester, or destroy the information and any copies it has. The option of sequestering or destroying the information is included in part because the receiving party may have incorporated the information in protected trial-preparation materials. No receiving party may use or disclose the information pending resolution of the privilege claim. The receiving party may present to the court the questions whether the information is privileged or protected as trial-preparation material, and whether the privilege or protection has been waived. If it does so, it must provide the court with the grounds for the privilege or protection specified in the producing party's notice, and serve all parties. In presenting the question, the party may use the content of the information only to the extent permitted by the applicable law of privilege, protection for trial-preparation material, and professional responsibility.

If a party disclosed the information to nonparties before receiving notice of a claim of privilege or protection as trial-preparation material, it must take reasonable steps to retrieve the information and to return it, sequester it until the claim is resolved, or destroy it.

Whether the information is returned or not, the producing party must preserve the information pending the court's ruling on whether the claim of privilege or of protection is properly asserted and whether it was waived. As with claims made under Rule 26(b)(5)(A), there may be no ruling if the other parties do not contest the claim.

Changes Made after Publication and Comment

The rule recommended for approval is modified from the published proposal. The rule is expanded to include trial-preparation protection claims in addition to privilege claims.

The published proposal referred to production "without intending to waive a claim of privilege." This reference to intent was deleted because many courts include intent in the factors that determine whether production waives privilege.

The published proposal required that the producing party give notice "within a reasonable time." The time requirement was deleted because it seemed to implicate the question whether production effected a waiver, a question not addressed by the rule, and also because a receiving party cannot practicably ignore a notice that it believes was unreasonably delayed. The notice procedure was further changed to require that the producing party state the basis for the claim.

Two statements in the published Note have been brought into the rule text. The first provides that the receiving party may not use or disclose the information until the claim is resolved. The second provides that if the receiving party disclosed the information before being notified, it must take reasonable steps to retrieve it.*

The rule text was expanded by adding a provision that the receiving party may promptly present the information to the court under seal for a determination of the claim.

The published proposal provided that the producing party must comply with Rule 26(b)(5)(A) after making the claim. This provision was deleted as unnecessary.

Changes are made in the Committee Note to reflect the changes in the rule text.

The changes from the published rule are shown below.

---

*In response to concerns about the proposal raised at the June 15-16, 2005, Standing Committee meeting, the Committee Note was revised to emphasize that the courts will continue to examine whether a privilege claim was made at a reasonable time, as part of substantive law.

Rule 26(b)(5)

Rule 26. General Provisions Governing Discovery; Duty of Disclosure*

* * * * *

(5) Claims of Privilege or Protection of Trial Preparation Materials.

(A) ~~Privileged i~~Information Withheld. When a party withholds information otherwise discoverable under these rules by claiming that it is privileged or subject to protection as trial preparation material, the party shall make the claim expressly and shall describe the nature of the documents, communications, or things not produced or disclosed in a manner that, without revealing information itself privileged or protected, will enable other parties to assess the applicability of the privilege or protection.

(B) ~~Privileged i~~Information Produced. If ~~When a party produces~~ information is produced in discovery that is subject to a claim of privilege or of protection as trial-preparation material, ~~without intending to waive a claim of privilege~~, the party making the claim ~~it~~ may~~, within a reasonable time,~~ notify any party that received the information of the claim and the basis for its ~~claim of privilege~~. After being notified, a party must promptly return, sequester, or destroy the specified information and

*Changes from the proposal published for public comment shown by double-underlining new material and striking through omitted matter.

54

any copies <u>it has and may not use or disclose the</u> <u>information until the claim is resolved.</u> A receiv<u>ing party may promptly present the information</u> <u>to the court under seal for a determination of the</u> <u>claim.</u> <u>If the receiving party disclosed the infor</u><u>mation before being notified, it must take reason</u><u>able steps to retrieve it.</u> The producing party must ~~comply with Rule 26(b)(5)(A) with regard to the~~ ~~information and~~ preserve ~~it~~ <u>the information until</u> <u>the</u> ~~privilege~~ <u>claim is resolved</u> ~~pending a ruling by~~ ~~the court~~.

iv. Interrogatories and Requests for Production Involving Electronically Stored Information: Rules 33 and 34(a) and (b)

Introduction

(a). Rule 33

The proposed amendment to Rule 33 clarifies how the option to produce business records to respond to an interrogatory operates in the information age. The rule is amended to make clear that the option to produce business records or make them available for examination, audit, or inspection, includes electronically stored information. The Note language clarifies how the limitation in Rule 33(d), permitting the production of records to respond to an interrogatory when "the burden of deriving or ascertaining the answer" is substantially the same for either party, applies to electronically stored information. The Note explains that depending on the circumstances, "the responding party may be required to provide some combination of technical support, information on application software, or other assistance" to enable the interrogating party to derive or ascertain the answer from the electronically stored information as readily as the responding party. In response to comments, the Note has been revised from the published version to clarify when such support might include direct access to a party's electronic information system. Because such access may raise sensitive problems of confidentiality or privacy, the Note states that the responding party may choose to derive or ascertain the answer itself.

(b).   Rule 34

The proposed amendment to Rule 34(a) adds "electronically stored information" as a category subject to production, in addition to "documents." Rule 34(b) is amended to add procedures for requesting and objecting to the form for producing such information and to provide "default" forms of production. Such requests and objections did not arise with paper discovery, because paper can generally be produced in only one form. By contrast, electronically stored information may exist in a number of different forms, some of which may be inappropriate for the litigation or costly or burdensome for the requesting or responding party.

Rule 34(a)

Adding "electronically stored information" to Rule 34(a)'s list of what is subject to production is an obvious change. In 1970, this list was revised to add "data or data compilations." This discovery rule revision was made to accommodate changes in technology; it is safe to say that the technological developments that prompted the 1970 amendment have been dwarfed by the revolution in information technology in the intervening decades, which we are grappling with today. The gap between the rule's present terminology and existing technology is exacerbated by the inclusion of "phonorecords" in the items subject to discovery and the reference to having to use "detection devices" to translate data or compilations into a usable form. Proposed revisions made since publication delete the archaic and redundant words "through detection devices," from the rule text. The term "electronically stored information" was further focused by addition of the word "stored" to Rule 34(a)(1), so that it speaks of information "stored" in any medium.

The public comments focused on whether "electronically stored information" should be included within the term "documents," or whether it should be a third category with "documents" and "things." The Committee heard that good arguments support both choices and that few negative consequences flow from either choice. The Committee decided to recommend making "electronically stored information" separate from "documents." Although courts and litigants have included such information in the word "documents" to make it discoverable under the present rule language, there are significant and growing differences that the distinction acknowledges. During the hearings, many technically sophisticated witnesses confirmed that significant types of electronically stored information — most notably dynamic databases — are extremely difficult to characterize as "documents." When the Advisory Committee decided in 1970 to include "data or data compilations" as a subset of "documents," the Committee expected that the rule would require a producing party to provide a "print-out of computer data." By contrast, while electronically stored information often can be produced in the form of a document, it also exists, and will more often be produced, in forms other than a document. Rather than continue to try to stretch the word "document" to make it fit this new category of stored information, the published proposed amendment to Rule 34 explicitly recognized electronically stored information as a separate category.

Some comments expressed concern that parties seeking production of "documents" under Rule 34 might not receive electronically stored information and would have to ask for it specifically. Note language responds to this concern. Even if a request refers only to documents — or to electronically stored information — the responding party must produce responsive information no matter what the storage form may be. In addition, the rules provide other steps that should alert a party to request electronically stored information if it is involved in a case. The parties are directed by Rule 26(f) to discuss discovery of electronically stored information if such discovery will occur in the case, and Rule 34(b) permits the requesting party to specify the form or forms for production of electronically stored information.

One other drafting matter with respect to Rule 34(a) deserves mention: the significance of the listed items in the parenthetical following the word "documents" in the current rule and the published draft. During the public comment period, some asked whether the listed items in that parenthetical refer only to "documents," and not "electronically stored information. The items listed refer, as applicable, to either or both electronically stored information and documents. For example, "data compilations" could be produced as paper, in a print-out of electronically stored information, or in electronic form; an "image" could be in a document or in an electronic form. The items listed reflect the breadth of both the terms "documents" and "electronically stored information." To clarify this point, redrafting after the public comment period reversed the order of "documents" and "electronically stored information" and changed the punctuation to replace the parentheses with a dash.

Rule 34(b)

Proposed amended Rule 34(b) provides a procedure for an issue that generally does not arise with paper discovery — electronically stored information exists and can be produced in a number of forms. The form or forms in which it is kept may not be a form that the requesting party can use or use efficiently or that the responding party wants to use for production. The form of producing electronically stored information is increasingly a source of dispute in discovery. The proposed amendment provides a structure and procedure for the parties to identify the form or forms of production that are most useful or appropriate for the litigation; provides guidance to the responding party if no request, order, or agreement specifies the form or forms of production; and provides guidance to the court if there is a dispute.

Proposed amended Rule 34(b) allows, but does not require, a requesting party to specify a form or forms for producing electronically stored information, clarifies that a responding party's objection to a request may include an objection to the specified form, requires a responding party to state the form or forms it intends to use for production in the written response it must file to the production request, and provides "default" forms of production to apply if the requesting party did not specify a form and there is no agreement or order requiring a particular form.

During the public comment period, concern was expressed as to the published language that described the so-called default forms of production. Rule 34(b), as published, stated that if the parties did not agree on forms of producing electronically stored information, and the court did not order specific forms of production, the responding party could produce in a "form in which it is ordinarily maintained, or in an electronically searchable form." These alternatives were intended to provide functional analogues to the existing rule language that provides choices for producing hard-copy documents: the form in which they are kept in the usual course of business or organized and labeled to correspond to the categories in the request. A number of commentators expressed concern that "a form ordinarily maintained" required "native format" production, which can have disadvantages ranging from an inability to redact, leading to privilege problems; an inability to bates-stamp the "document" for purposes of litigation management and control, which is not an insignificant consideration, particularly in complex multi-party cases; and the receiving party's ability to create "documents" from the produced native format data and present them back to the producing party as deposition or proposed trial exhibits that, while based on the native format data produced, are totally unfamiliar to the producing party. The commentators expressed concern that the alternative provided, an "electronically searchable form," might exert pressure for "native format" production due to the difficulties that attend providing an electronically searchable form. Other comments challenged this alternative default as a standard that should not be applied for all cases. A form that is readily searchable on one party's system may not be easily searched, or searched at all, on another party's system. And there is a converse concern that the requesting party might insist on production in a form searchable in its own unique system, imposing undue conversion costs on the producing party. Other information may exist in an electronic form that is not searchable in any meaningful sense. Requiring electronic searchability, moreover, may be unnecessary or even unwanted in some cases. Many parties continue to seek and provide information in paper form by printing out electronic files. On the other hand, commentators noted that it is important to frame the rule to provide the same kind of protection against discovery abuse that is provided for paper discovery by the present choice between producing documents as they are kept in the usual course of business or organized and labelled to correspond with the categories in the request. Producing electronically stored information with the ability to search by electronic means removed or degraded is the electronic discovery version of the "document dump," the production of large amounts of paper with no organization or order.

In response to these and other concerns, rule and Note language have been revised. The existing language of Rule 34(a) provided the starting point, by requiring a responding party to "translate" electronic information, if necessary, "into reasonably usable form." The Committee was concerned in its discussion that the Rule 34(b) "default" forms of production should be consistent with this Rule 34(a) requirement. After discussion, the Committee decided to retain the published rule language that one default form of production be the form or forms in which the responding party ordinarily maintains the information, but to make the alternative "a form or forms that are reasonably usable." Under Rule 34(a) and (b), the form or forms in which the responding party ordinarily maintains its information can be the default choice of the responding party, but if necessary that party might have to translate the information to make it "reasonably usable." Or the responding party can choose a form that it does not ordinarily use, as long as it is reasonably usable. This is consistent with Rule 34(a) as it has stood since 1970.

If the information is maintained in a way that is not usable by anyone – for example, it may be stored on obsolete sources or require equipment that is unavailable – the problem is properly addressed under Rule 26(b)(2), which covers electronically stored information that is not reasonably accessible. If the requesting party has esoteric or idiosyncratic features on its information system that would be unduly burdensome or costly for the responding party to accommodate, producing the information in a form that can be used with software that is in general commercial use should be "reasonably usable."

During the comment period, as noted, concerns were raised about whether the "default forms" of production would permit responding parties to produce electronically stored information in ways that remove or degrade functions that are useful to the requesting party, such as features that make it electronically searchable. Committee Note language responds to this concern, stating that the option to produce in a reasonably usable form does not mean that a responding party is free to convert electronically stored information from the form in which it is ordinarily maintained to a different form that makes it more difficult or burdensome for the requesting party to use the information efficiently in the litigation. If the responding party ordinarily maintains the

Rules 33 & 34

information it is producing in a way that makes it searchable by electronic means, the information should not be produced in a form that removes or significantly degrades this feature.

Rule 34(b) was changed from the published version to permit the parties to specify the form "or forms" for production of electronically stored information. This change recognizes the fact that different types of information may best be produced in different forms. In addition, the provision stating that a producing party need produce the same electronically stored information in only one form was relocated to make it clear that this limitation applies when the requesting party specifies the desired form or forms in the request.

The Proposed Rules and Committee Notes

Rule 33

The Committee recommends approval of the following amendment:

Rule 33. Interrogatories to Parties

* * * * *

(d) Option to Produce Business Records. Where the answer to an interrogatory may be derived or ascertained from the business records, including electronically stored information, of the party upon whom the interrogatory has been served or from an examination, audit or inspection of such business records, including a compilation, abstract or summary thereof, and the burden of deriving or ascertaining the answer is substantially the same for the party serving the interrogatory as for the party served, it is a sufficient answer to such interrogatory to specify the records from which the answer may be derived or ascertained and to afford to the party serving the interrogatory reasonable opportunity to examine, audit or inspect such records and to make copies, compilations, abstracts, or summaries. A specification shall be in sufficient detail to permit the interrogating party to locate and to identify, as readily as can the party served, the records from which the answer may be ascertained.

* * * * *

Committee Note

Rule 33(d) is amended to parallel Rule 34(a) by recognizing the importance of electronically stored information. The term "electronically stored information" has the same broad meaning in Rule 33(d) as in Rule 34(a). Much business information is stored only in electronic form; the Rule 33(d) option should be available with respect to such records as well.

Special difficulties may arise in using electronically stored information, either due to its form or because it is dependent on a particular computer system. Rule 33(d) allows a responding party to substitute access to documents or electronically stored information for an answer only if the burden of deriving the answer will be substantially the same for either party. Rule 33(d) states that a party electing to respond to an interrogatory by providing electronically stored information must ensure that the interrogating party can locate and identify it "as readily as can the party served," and that the responding party must give the interrogating party a "reasonable opportunity to examine, audit, or inspect" the information. Depending on the circumstances, satisfying these provisions with regard to electronically stored information may require the responding party to provide some combination of technical support, information on application software, or other assistance. The key question is whether such support enables the interrogating party to derive or ascertain the answer from the electronically stored information as readily as the responding party. A party that wishes to invoke Rule 33(d) by specifying electronically stored information may be required to provide direct access to its electronic information system, but only if that is necessary to afford the requesting party an adequate opportunity to derive or ascertain the answer to the interrogatory. In that situation, the responding party's need to protect sensitive interests of confidentiality or privacy may mean that it must derive or ascertain and provide the answer itself rather than invoke Rule 33(d).

Changes Made after Publication and Comment

No changes are made to the rule text. The Committee Note is changed to reflect the sensitivities that limit direct access by a requesting party to a responding party's information system. If direct access to the responding party's system is the only way to enable a requesting party to locate and identify the records from which the answer may be ascertained, the responding party may choose to derive or ascertain the answer itself.

Rule 34

The Committee recommends the following rule amendment and accompanying Committee Note:

Rule 34. Production of Documents, Electronically Stored Information, and Things and Entry Upon Land for Inspection and Other Purposes

(a) Scope. Any party may serve on any other party a request (1) to produce and permit the party making the request, or someone acting on the requestor's behalf, to inspect, ~~and~~ copy, test, or sample any designated documents or electronically stored information — (including writings, drawings, graphs, charts, photographs, sound recordings, images ~~phonorecords~~, and other data or data compilations stored in any medium from which information can be obtained; — translated, if necessary, by the respondent ~~through detection devices~~ into reasonably usable form), or to inspect, ~~and~~ copy, test, or sample any designated tangible things which constitute or contain matters within the scope of Rule 26(b) and which are in the possession, custody or control of the party upon whom the request is served; or (2) to permit entry upon designated land or other property in the possession or control of the party upon whom the request is served for the purpose of inspection and measuring, surveying, photographing, testing, or sampling the property or any designated object or operation thereon, within the scope of Rule 26(b).

(b) Procedure. The request shall set forth, either by individual item or by category, the items to be inspected, and describe each with reasonable particularity. The request shall specify a reasonable time, place, and manner of making the inspection and performing the related acts. The request may specify the form or forms in which electronically stored information is to be produced. Without leave of court or written stipulation, a request may not be served before the time specified in Rule 26(d).

The party upon whom the request is served shall serve a written response within 30 days after the service of the request. A shorter or longer time may be directed by the court or, in the absence of such an order, agreed to in writing by the parties, subject to Rule 29. The response shall state, with respect to each item or category, that inspection and related activities will be permitted as requested, unless the request is objected to, including an objection to the requested form or forms for producing electronically stored information, ~~in which event~~ stating the reasons for the objection ~~shall be stated~~. If objection is made to part of an item or category, the part shall be specified and inspection permitted of the remaining parts. If objection is made to the requested form or forms for producing electronically stored information – or if no form was specified in the request – the responding party must state the form or forms it intends to use. The party submitting the request may move for an order under Rule 37(a) with respect to any objection to or other failure to respond to the request or any part thereof, or any failure to permit inspection as requested.

Unless the parties otherwise agree, or the court otherwise orders:

(i) ~~A~~a party who produces documents for inspection shall produce them as they are kept in the usual course of business or shall organize and label them to correspond with the categories in the request~~.~~;

(ii) if a request does not specify the form or forms for producing electronically stored information, a responding party must produce the information in a form or forms in which it is ordinarily maintained or in a form or forms that are reasonably usable; and

(iii) a party need not produce the same electronically stored information in more than one form.

* * * * *

Committee Note

Subdivision (a). As originally adopted, Rule 34 focused on discovery of "documents" and "things." In 1970, Rule 34(a) was amended to include discovery of data compilations, anticipating that the use of computerized information would increase. Since then, the growth in electronically stored information and in the variety of systems for creating and storing such information has been dramatic. Lawyers and judges interpreted the term "documents" to include electronically stored information because it was obviously improper to allow a party to evade discovery obligations on the basis that the label had not kept pace with changes in information technology. But it has become increasingly difficult to say that all forms of electronically stored information, many dynamic in nature, fit within the traditional concept of a "document." Electronically stored information may exist in dynamic databases and other forms far different from fixed expression on paper. Rule 34(a) is amended to confirm that discovery of electronically stored information stands on equal footing with discovery of paper documents. The change clarifies that Rule 34 applies to information that is fixed in a tangible form and to information that is stored in a medium from which it can be retrieved and examined. At the same time, a Rule 34 request for production of "documents" should be understood to encompass, and the response should include, electronically stored information unless discovery in the action has clearly distinguished between electronically stored information and "documents."

Discoverable information often exists in both paper and electronic form, and the same or similar information might exist in both. The items listed in Rule 34(a) show different ways in which information may be recorded or stored. Images, for example, might be hard-copy documents or electronically stored information. The wide variety of computer systems currently in use, and the rapidity of technological change, counsel against a limiting or precise definition of electronically stored information. Rule 34(a)(1) is expansive and includes any type of information that is stored electronically. A common example often sought in discovery is electronic communications, such as e-mail. The rule covers — either as documents or as electronically stored information — information "stored in any medium," to encompass future developments in computer technology. Rule 34(a)(1) is intended to be broad enough to cover all current types of computer-based information, and flexible enough to encompass future changes and developments.

Rules 33 & 34

References elsewhere in the rules to "electronically stored information" should be understood to invoke this expansive approach. A companion change is made to Rule 33(d), making it explicit that parties choosing to respond to an interrogatory by permitting access to responsive records may do so by providing access to electronically stored information. More generally, the term used in Rule 34(a)(1) appears in a number of other amendments, such as those to Rules 26(a)(1), 26(b)(2), 26(b)(5)(B), 26(f), 34(b), 37(f), and 45. In each of these rules, electronically stored information has the same broad meaning it has under Rule 34(a)(1). References to "documents" appear in discovery rules that are not amended, including Rules 30(f), 36(a), and 37(c)(2). These references should be interpreted to include electronically stored information as circumstances warrant.

The term "electronically stored information" is broad, but whether material that falls within this term should be produced, and in what form, are separate questions that must be addressed under Rules 26(b), 26(c), and 34(b).

The Rule 34(a) requirement that, if necessary, a party producing electronically stored information translate it into reasonably usable form does not address the issue of translating from one human language to another. See In re Puerto Rico Elect. Power Auth., 687 F.2d 501, 504-510 (1st Cir. 1989).

Rule 34(a)(1) is also amended to make clear that parties may request an opportunity to test or sample materials sought under the rule in addition to inspecting and copying them. That opportunity may be important for both electronically stored information and hard-copy materials. The current rule is not clear that such testing or sampling is authorized; the amendment expressly permits it. As with any other form of discovery, issues of burden and intrusiveness raised by requests to test or sample can be addressed under Rules 26(b)(2) and 26(c). Inspection or testing of certain types of electronically stored information or of a responding party's electronic information system may raise issues of confidentiality or privacy. The addition of testing and sampling to Rule 34(a) with regard to documents and electronically stored information is not meant to create a routine right of direct access to a party's electronic information system, although such access might be justified in some circumstances. Courts should guard against undue intrusiveness resulting from inspecting or testing such systems.

Rule 34(a)(1) is further amended to make clear that tangible things must — like documents and land sought to be examined — be designated in the request.

Subdivision (b). Rule 34(b) provides that a party must produce documents as they are kept in the usual course of business or must organize and label them to correspond with the categories in the discovery request. The production of electronically stored information should be subject to comparable requirements to protect against deliberate or inadvertent production in ways that raise unnecessary obstacles for the requesting party. Rule 34(b) is amended to ensure similar protection for electronically stored information.

Rules 33 & 34

The amendment to Rule 34(b) permits the requesting party to designate the form or forms in which it wants electronically stored information produced. The form of production is more important to the exchange of electronically stored information than of hard-copy materials, although a party might specify hard copy as the requested form. Specification of the desired form or forms may facilitate the orderly, efficient, and cost-effective discovery of electronically stored information. The rule recognizes that different forms of production may be appropriate for different types of electronically stored information. Using current technology, for example, a party might be called upon to produce word processing documents, e-mail messages, electronic spreadsheets, different image or sound files, and material from databases. Requiring that such diverse types of electronically stored information all be produced in the same form could prove impossible, and even if possible could increase the cost and burdens of producing and using the information. The rule therefore provides that the requesting party may ask for different forms of production for different types of electronically stored information.

The rule does not require that the requesting party choose a form or forms of production. The requesting party may not have a preference. In some cases, the requesting party may not know what form the producing party uses to maintain its electronically stored information, although Rule 26(f)(3) is amended to call for discussion of the form of production in the parties' prediscovery conference.

The responding party also is involved in determining the form of production. In the written response to the production request that Rule 34 requires, the responding party must state the form it intends to use for producing electronically stored information if the requesting party does not specify a form or if the responding party objects to a form that the requesting party specifies. Stating the intended form before the production occurs may permit the parties to identify and seek to resolve disputes before the expense and work of the production occurs. A party that responds to a discovery request by simply producing electronically stored information in a form of its choice, without identifying that form in advance of the production in the response required by Rule 34(b), runs a risk that the requesting party can show that the produced form is not reasonably usable and that it is entitled to production of some or all of the information in an additional form. Additional time might be required to permit a responding party to assess the appropriate form or forms of production.

If the requesting party is not satisfied with the form stated by the responding party, or if the responding party has objected to the form specified by the requesting party, the parties must meet and confer under Rule 37(a)(2)(B) in an effort to resolve the matter before the requesting party can file a motion to compel. If they cannot agree and the court resolves the dispute, the court is not limited to the forms initially chosen by the requesting party, stated by the responding party, or specified in this rule for situations in which there is no court order or party agreement.

If the form of production is not specified by party agreement or court order, the responding party must produce electronically stored information either in a form or forms in which it is ordinarily maintained or in a form or forms that are reasonably usable. Rule 34(a) requires that, if necessary, a responding party "translate" information it produces into a "reasonably usable" form. Under some circumstances, the responding party may need to provide some reasonable amount of technical support, information on application software, or other reasonable assistance to enable the requesting party to use the information. The rule does not require a party to produce electronically stored information in the form it which it is ordinarily maintained, as long as it is produced in a reasonably usable form. But the option to produce in a reasonably usable form does not mean that a responding party is free to convert electronically stored information from the form in which it is ordinarily maintained to a different form that makes it more difficult or burdensome for the requesting party to use the information efficiently in the litigation. If the responding party ordinarily maintains the information it is producing in a way that makes it searchable by electronic means, the information should not be produced in a form that removes or significantly degrades this feature.

Some electronically stored information may be ordinarily maintained in a form that is not reasonably usable by any party. One example is "legacy" data that can be used only by superseded systems. The questions whether a producing party should be required to convert such information to a more usable form, or should be required to produce it at all, should be addressed under Rule 26(b)(2)(B).

Whether or not the requesting party specified the form of production, Rule 34(b) provides that the same electronically stored information ordinarily need be produced in only one form.

Changes Made after Publication and Comment

The proposed amendment recommended for approval has been modified from the published version. The sequence of "documents or electronically stored information" is changed to emphasize that the parenthetical exemplifications apply equally to illustrate "documents" and "electronically stored information." The reference to "detection devices" is deleted as redundant with "translated" and as archaic.

The references to the form of production are changed in the rule and Committee Note to refer also to "forms." Different forms may be appropriate or necessary for different sources of information.

The published proposal allowed the requesting party to specify a form for production and recognized that the responding party could object to the requested form. This procedure is now amplified by directing that the responding party state the form or forms it intends to use for production if the request does not specify a form or if the responding party objects to the requested form.

The default forms of production to be used when the parties do not agree on a form and there is no court order are changed in part. As in the published proposal, one default form is "a form or forms in which [electronically stored information] is ordinarily maintained." The alternative default form, however, is changed from "an electronically searchable

Rules 33 & 34

form" to "a form or forms that are reasonably usable." "[A]n electronically searchable form" proved to have several defects. Some electronically stored information cannot be searched electronically. In addition, there often are many different levels of electronic searchability — the published default would authorize production in a minimally searchable form even though more easily searched forms might be available at equal or less cost to the responding party.

The provision that absent court order a party need not produce the same electronically stored information in more than one form was moved to become a separate item for the sake of emphasis.

The Committee Note was changed to reflect these changes in rule text, and also to clarify many aspects of the published Note. In addition, the Note was expanded to add a caveat to the published amendment that establishes the rule that documents — and now electronically stored information — may be tested and sampled as well as inspected and copied. Fears were expressed that testing and sampling might imply routine direct access to a party's information system. The Note states that direct access is not a routine right, "although such access might be justified in some circumstances."

The changes in the rule text since publication are set out below.

Rule 34. Production of Documents, Electronically Stored Information, and Things and Entry Upon Land for Inspection and Other Purposes[*]

(a) Scope. Any party may serve on any other party a request (1) to produce and permit the party making the request, or someone acting on the requestor's behalf, to inspect, copy, test, or sample any designated documents or electronically stored information or any designated documents (– including writings, drawings, graphs, charts, photographs, sound recordings, images, and other data or data compilations stored in any medium – from which information can be obtained, translated, if necessary, by the respondent through detection devices into reasonably usable form), . . .

* * * * *

(b) Procedure. The request shall set forth, either by indi-

*Changes from the proposal published for public comment shown by double-underlining new material and striking through omitted matter.

vidual item or by category, the items to be inspected, and describe each with reasonable particularity. The request shall specify a reasonable time, place, and manner of making the inspection and performing the related acts. The request may specify the form <u>or forms</u> in which electronically stored information is to be produced.

* * * * *

The response shall state, with respect to each item or category, that inspection and related activities will be permitted as requested, unless the request is objected to, including an objection to the requested form <u>or forms</u> for producing electronically stored information, stating the reasons for the objection. If objection is made to part of an item or category, the part shall be specified and inspection permitted of the remaining parts. <u>If objection is made to the requested form or forms for producing electronically stored information — or if no form was specified in the request — the responding party must state the form or forms it intends to use.</u> The party submitting the request may move for an order under Rule 37(a) with respect to any objection to or other failure to respond to the request or any part thereof, or any failure to permit inspection as requested.

Unless the parties otherwise agree, or the court otherwise orders,

* * * * *

(ii) if a request for electronically stored information does not specify the form <u>or forms</u> of production, a responding party must produce the information in a form <u>or forms</u> in which it is ordinarily maintained or in ~~an electronically searchable form~~ <u>a form or forms that are reasonably usable;</u> ~~The party need only produce such information in one form.~~ <u>and</u>

<u>**(iii)** a party need not produce the same electronically stored information in more than one form.</u>

v. Sanctions for a Certain Type of Loss of Electronically Stored Information: Rule 37(f)

Introduction

Proposed Rule 37(f) responds to a distinctive feature of electronic information systems, the routine modification, overwriting, and deletion of information that attends normal use. The proposed rule provides limited protection against sanctions for a party's inability to provide electronically stored information in discovery when that information has been lost as a result of the routine operation of an electronic information system, as long as that operation is in good faith.

Examples of this feature in present systems include programs that recycle storage media kept for brief periods against the possibility of a disaster that broadly affects computer operations; automatic overwriting of information that has been "deleted"; programs that change metadata (automatically created identifying information about the history or management of an electronic file) to reflect the latest access to particular electronically stored information; and programs that automatically discard information that has not been accessed within a defined period or that exists beyond a defined period without an affirmative effort to store it for a longer period. Similarly, many database programs automatically create, discard, or update information without specific direction from, or awareness of, users. By protecting against sanctions for loss of information as a result of the routine operation of a computer system, the proposed rule recognizes that such automatic features are essential to the operation of electronic information systems. The proposed rule also recognizes that suspending or interrupting these features can be prohibitively expensive and burdensome, again in ways that have no counterpart to managing hard-copy information. One reason is that hard-copy document retention and destruction programs are not intertwined with, nor an inextricable part of, ongoing business processes. A data producer can warehouse large volumes of papers without affecting ongoing activities and can maintain and manage hard-copy records separately from the creation of products or services. By contrast, electronic information is usually part of the data producer's activities, whether it be the manufacture of products or the provision of services. It can be difficult to interrupt the routine operation of computer systems to isolate and preserve discrete parts of the information they overwrite, delete, or update on an ongoing basis, without creating problems for the larger system. It is unrealistic to expect parties to stop such routine operation of their computer systems as soon as they anticipate litigation. It is also undesirable; the result would be even greater accumulation of duplicative and irrelevant data that must be reviewed, making discovery more expensive and time-consuming. There is considerable uncertainty as to whether a party — particularly a party that produces large amounts of information — nonetheless has to interrupt the operation of the electronic information systems it is using to avoid any loss of information because of the possibility that it might be sought in discovery, or risk severe sanctions.

Proposed Rule 37(f) is not intended to provide a shield for parties that intentionally destroy information because of its relationship to litigation by, for example, exploiting the routine operation of an information system to target specific electronically stored information for destruction in order to avoid producing that information in discovery. Defining the culpability standard that would make a party ineligible for protection under Rule 37(f) presented a challenge. Rule 37(f) was therefore published in two versions and the Committee particularly invited commentary on the appropriate culpability standard. The text version adopted essentially a negligence test, requiring that the party seeking protection under the proposed rule have taken reasonable steps to preserve information after it knew the information was discoverable in the action. A footnote offered an alternative version setting a higher culpability threshold — that sanctions could not be imposed unless the party intentionally or recklessly failed to preserve the information. Both versions of the published Rule 37(f) draft also precluded protection when the loss of the information violated a court order.

Much public commentary focused on Rule 37(f). A number of comments urged that the text version — precluding any protection under the rule even for negligent loss of information — provided no meaningful protection, but rather protected against conduct unlikely to be sanctioned in the first place. Any mistake in interrupting the routine operation of a computer system might be found not reasonable, defeating application of the rule. Others urged that the footnote version was too restrictive. Proving that a litigant acted intentionally or recklessly in permitting the regular operation of an information system to continue might prove quite difficult and require discovery and fact-finding that could involve inquiry into difficult subjective issues. Adopting the footnote version could insulate conduct that should be subject to sanctions.

Public commentary also focused on the court-order provision included in both published drafts. Many argued that this provision would promote

Rules 37(f)

applications for preservation orders as a way to defeat application of the proposed rule. Others urged that the court-order provision be narrowed to orders that "specifically" called for preservation of certain electronically stored information, for fear that broad preservation orders would nullify the Rule 37(f) protection altogether.

Public commentary also emphasized the possible relationship between Rule 37(f) and the proposed amendment to Rule 26(b)(2) that — unless the court orders discovery — excuses a responding party from providing discovery of electronically stored information that is not reasonably accessible. Many commentators expressed a concern or expectation that the interaction of Rules 26(b)(2) and 37(f) meant that absent a preservation order, there would be no obligation to preserve information a party contended was not reasonably accessible because such information was not "discoverable" under Rule 26(b)(2).

The Advisory Committee carefully considered the comments and made adjustments in the rule and the Note to respond to them. It retained the fundamental focus on the routine operation of an electronic information system. But it revised Rule 37(f) to adopt a culpability standard intermediate between the two published versions. The proposed rule provides protection from sanctions only for the "good faith" routine operation of an electronic information system.

As the Note explains, good faith may require that a party intervene to suspend certain features of the routine operation of an information system to prevent loss of information subject to preservation obligations. Such intervention is often called a "litigation hold." The rule itself does not purport to create or affect such preservation obligations, but recognizes that they may arise from many sources, including common law, statutes, and regulations. The steps taken to implement an effective litigation hold bear on good faith, as does compliance with any agreements the parties have reached regarding preservation and with any court orders directing preservation. Such party agreements may emerge from the early discovery-planning conference, which the proposed amendments to Rule 26(f) provide should include discussion of preserving discoverable information.

The revised rule also includes a provision that permits sanctions in "exceptional circumstances" even when information is lost because of a party's good-faith routine operation of a computer system. The exceptional circumstances provision adds flexibility not included in the published drafts.

The Advisory Committee also decided that the court-order provision should be removed from the rule. Many comments noted that the provision would create an incentive to obtain a preservation order to make the rule's protection unavailable. As stated in the Note to Rule 26(f) (regarding the discussion of preservation during the discovery-planning conference), preservation orders should not be routinely entered. The existence of a court order remains important, however; as the Rule 37(f) Note recognizes, steps taken to comply with orders calling for preservation of information bear on the good faith of a party that has lost information due to the routine operation of a computer system.

To respond to concerns that the proposed rule would insulate routine destruction of information on sources a party identifies as not reasonably accessible, the Notes to both Rules 37(f) and 26(b)(2) have been revised to make clear that there is no necessary linkage between these rules. Thus, the Rule 37(f) Note says that good faith may require preservation of information on sources a party believes are not reasonably accessible under Rule 26(b)(2).

In addition, the Advisory Committee changed the reference to routine operation from "a party's" information system to "an" information system. This change recognizes that in many cases, a party's electronically stored information is actually stored on a system owned by another, such as a vendor in a contractual relationship with the party. Absent this change, the rule could result in holding a party subject to sanctions for the loss of information resulting from the routine, good-faith operation of a computer system because the information was on a system operated by a vendor or other entity. The rule continues to focus on the party's good faith in the operation of a system containing the party's information. For example, if a party stored certain electronically stored information on a vendor's computer system and that information became subject to a preservation obligation, the party's good faith would be measured by its efforts to arrange for the preservation of the information on that system.

The Proposed Rule and Committee Note

Rule 37(f)

The Committee recommends approval of the following proposed amendment:

Rule 37. Failure to Make Disclosures or Cooperate in Discovery; Sanctions

* * * * *

(f) Electronically stored information. Absent exceptional circumstances, a court may not impose sanctions under these rules on a party for failing to provide electronically stored

Rule 37(f)

<u>information lost as a result of the routine, good-faith operation of an electronic information system.</u>

Committee Note

Subdivision (f). Subdivision (f) is new. It focuses on a distinctive feature of computer operations, the routine alteration and deletion of information that attends ordinary use. Many steps essential to computer operation may alter or destroy information, for reasons that have nothing to do with how that information might relate to litigation. As a result, the ordinary operation of computer systems creates a risk that a party may lose potentially discoverable information without culpable conduct on its part. Under Rule 37(f), absent exceptional circumstances, sanctions cannot be imposed for loss of electronically stored information resulting from the routine, good-faith operation of an electronic information system.

Rule 37(f) applies only to information lost due to the "routine operation of an electronic information system" — the ways in which such systems are generally designed, programmed, and implemented to meet the party's technical and business needs. The "routine operation" of computer systems includes the alteration and overwriting of information, often without the operator's specific direction or awareness, a feature with no direct counterpart in hard-copy documents. Such features are essential to the operation of electronic information systems.

Rule 37(f) applies to information lost due to the routine operation of an information system only if the operation was in good faith. Good faith in the routine operation of an information system may involve a party's intervention to modify or suspend certain features of that routine operation to prevent the loss of information, if that information is subject to a preservation obligation. A preservation obligation may arise from many sources, including common law, statutes, regulations, or a court order in the case. The good faith requirement of Rule 37(f) means that a party is not permitted to exploit the routine operation of an information system to thwart discovery obligations by allowing that operation to continue in order to destroy specific stored information that it is required to preserve. When a party is under a duty to preserve information because of pending or reasonably anticipated litigation, intervention in the routine operation of an information system is one aspect of what is often called a "litigation hold." Among the factors that bear on a party's good faith in the routine operation of an information system are the steps the party took to comply with a court order in the case or party agreement requiring preservation of specific electronically stored information.

Whether good faith would call for steps to prevent the loss of information on sources that the party believes are not reasonably accessible under Rule 26(b)(2) depends on the circumstances of each case. One factor is whether the party reasonably believes that the information on such sources is likely to be discoverable and not available from reasonably accessible sources.

The protection provided by Rule 37(f) applies only to sanctions "under

Rule 37(f)

these rules." It does not affect other sources of authority to impose sanctions or rules of professional responsibility.

This rule restricts the imposition of "sanctions." It does not prevent a court from making the kinds of adjustments frequently used in managing discovery if a party is unable to provide relevant responsive information. For example, a court could order the responding party to produce an additional witness for deposition, respond to additional interrogatories, or make similar attempts to provide substitutes or alternatives for some or all of the lost information.

Changes Made after Publication and Comment

The published rule barred sanctions only if the party who lost electronically stored information took reasonable steps to preserve the information after it knew or should have known the information was discoverable in the action. A footnote invited comment on an alternative standard that barred sanctions unless the party recklessly or intentionally failed to preserve the information. The present proposal establishes an intermediate standard, protecting against sanctions if the information was lost in the "good faith" operation of an electronic information system. The present proposal carries forward a related element that was a central part of the published proposal — the information must have been lost in the system's "routine operation." The change to a good-faith test made it possible to eliminate the reference to information "discoverable in the action," removing a potential source of confusion as to the duty to preserve information on sources that are identified as not reasonably accessible under Rule 26(b)(2)(B).

The change to a good-faith standard is accompanied by addition of a provision that permits sanctions for loss of information in good-faith routine operation in "exceptional circumstances." This provision recognizes that in some circumstances a court should provide remedies to protect an entirely innocent party requesting discovery against serious prejudice arising from the loss of potentially important information.

As published, the rule included an express exception that denied protection if a party "violated an order in the action requiring it to preserve electronically stored information." This exception was deleted for fear that it would invite routine applications for preservation orders, and often for overbroad orders. The revised Committee Note observes that violation of an order is an element in determining whether a party acted in good faith.

The revised proposal broadens the rule's protection by applying to operation of "an" electronic information system, rather than "the party's" system. The change protects a party who has contracted with an outside firm to provide electronic information storage, avoiding potential arguments whether the system can be characterized as "the party's." The party remains obliged to act in good faith to avoid loss of information in routine operations conducted by the outside firm.

The Committee Note is changed to reflect the changes in the rule text.

Rule 37(f)

The changes from the published version of the proposed rule text are set out below.

Rule 37. Failure to Make Disclosures or Cooperate in Discovery; Sanctions[*]

* * * * *

(f) Electronically Stored Information. <u>Absent exceptional circumstances,</u> ~~Unless a party violated an order in the action requiring it to preserve electronically stored information,~~ <u>a</u> court may not impose sanctions under these rules on a ~~the~~ party for failing to provide ~~such~~ <u>electronically stored information lost as a result of the routine, good-faith operation of an electronic information system.</u> ~~if:~~

~~(1) the party took reasonable steps to preserve the information after it knew or should have known the information was discoverable in the action; and~~

~~(2) the failure resulted from loss of the information because of the routine operation of the party's electronic information system.~~

* * * * *

vi.   Rule 45

Introduction

Rule 45 provisions for subpoenas to produce documents apply to electronically stored information as well as traditional paper documents. The published amendments proposed revisions designed to keep Rule 45 in line with the other amendments addressing electronically stored information. Virtually all of the public comment and testimony focused on the other amendments. It was assumed that Rule 45 would conform, where appropriate, to any changes proposed for the other rules. A description of the changes made since publication serves also to describe the Rule 45 amendments in general.

A simple change was to expand the Rule 45(a)(1) provision that a

---

[*]Changes from the proposal published for public comment shown by double-underlining new material and striking through omitted matter.

subpoena may specify the form for producing electronically stored information to include the "forms." This change parallels changes made in Rules 26(f) and 34. The same change is made in the Rule 45(c)(2)(B) provision for objecting to the form or forms requested in the subpoena and in the Rule 45(d)(1)(B) provision for the default form or forms of production.

Similarly, the default form of the production provision was changed to accord with revised Rule 34(b), dropping the alternative for "an electronically searchable form" and substituting a form or forms that are "reasonably usable."

The Rule 45(d)(1)(E) provision protecting against production of electronically stored information that is not reasonably accessible was revised to mirror the changes made in Rule 26(b)(2)(B). The producing person must identify the sources, not the information; "undue burden or cost" is added to provide a test of reasonable accessibility; motions both to compel discovery and to quash are expressly recognized; discovery of information not reasonably accessible is allowed on court order after finding good cause, considering the limitations of Rule 26(b)(2)(C); and the court's authority to specify conditions for discovery is expressly stated.

Several changes were made in the Rule 45(d)(2)(B) provision that tracks the Rule 26(b)(5)(B) provision for asserting a claim of privilege after information is produced. Trial-preparation material is added to this procedure. The person making the claim must state the basis for the claim. The party receiving the information may not use or disclose it until the claim is resolved, but may present it to the court under seal for a determination of the claim. The receiving party also must take reasonable steps to retrieve the information if it was disclosed to others.

The Proposed Rule and Committee Note

Rule 45

The Committee recommends approval of amendments to Rule 45 that incorporate the corresponding changes made to the discovery rules.

Rule 45. Subpoena

(a) Form; Issuance.

(1) Every subpoena shall

(A) state the name of the court from which it is issued; and

(B) state the title of the action, the name of the

court in which it is pending, and its civil action number; and

(C) command each person to whom it is directed to attend and give testimony or to produce and permit inspection, ~~and~~ copying, testing, or sampling of designated books, documents, electronically stored information, or tangible things in the possession, custody or control of that person, or to permit inspection of premises, at a time and place therein specified; and

(D) set forth the text of subdivisions (c) and (d) of this rule.

A command to produce evidence or to permit inspection, copying, testing, or sampling may be joined with a command to appear at trial or hearing or at deposition, or may be issued separately. A subpoena may specify the form or forms in which electronically stored information is to be produced.

(2)[*] A subpoena must issue as follows:

* * * * *

(C) for production, ~~and~~ inspection, copying, testing, or sampling, if separate from a subpoena commanding a person's attendance, from the court for the district where the production or inspection is to be made.

(3) The clerk shall issue a subpoena, signed but otherwise in blank, to a party requesting it, who shall complete it before service. An attorney as officer of

---

[*] Amendments to subdivision (a)(2) are due to take effect on December 1, 2005.

the court may also issue and sign a subpoena on behalf of

    (A) a court in which the attorney is authorized to practice; or

    (B) a court for a district in which a deposition or production is compelled by the subpoena, if the deposition or production pertains to an action pending in a court in which the attorney is authorized to practice.

(b) Service.

  (1) A subpoena may be served by any person who is not a party and is not less than 18 years of age. Service of a subpoena upon a person named therein shall be made by delivering a copy thereof to such person and, if the person's attendance is commanded, by tendering to that person the fees for one day's attendance and the mileage allowed by law. When the subpoena is issued on behalf of the United States or an officer or agency thereof, fees and mileage need not be tendered. Prior notice of any commanded production of documents and things or inspection of premises before trial shall be served on each party in the manner prescribed by Rule 5(b).

  (2) Subject to the provisions of clause (ii) of subparagraph (c)(3)(A) of this rule, a subpoena may be served at any place within the district of the court by which it is issued, or at any place without the district that is within 100 miles of the place of the deposition, hearing, trial, production, ~~or~~ inspection, <u>copying, testing, or sampling</u> specified in the subpoena or at any place within the state where a state statute or rule of court permits service of a subpoena issued by a state court of general jurisdiction sitting in the place of the deposition, hearing, trial, production, ~~or~~ inspection, copying, testing, or sampling specified in the subpoena. When a statute of the United States provides therefor, the court upon proper application and cause shown may authorize the service of a subpoena at any other place. A subpoena directed to a witness in a foreign country who is a national or resident of the United States shall issue under the circumstances and in the manner and be served as provided in Title 28, U.S.C. § 1783.

(3) Proof of service when necessary shall be made by filing with the clerk of the court by which the subpoena is issued a statement of the date and manner of service and of the names of the persons served, certified by the person who made the service.

(c) Protection of Persons Subject to Subpoenas.

(1) A party or an attorney responsible for the issuance and service of a subpoena shall take reasonable steps to avoid imposing undue burden or expense on a person subject to that subpoena. The court on behalf of which the subpoena was issued shall enforce this duty and impose upon the party or attorney in breach of this duty an appropriate sanction, which may include, but is not limited to, lost earnings and a reasonable attorney's fee.

(2)(A) A person commanded to produce and permit inspection, ~~and~~ copying, testing, or sampling of designated electronically stored information, books, papers, documents or tangible things, or inspection of premises need not appear in person at the place of production or inspection unless commanded to appear for deposition, hearing or trial.

(B) Subject to paragraph (d)(2) of this rule, a person commanded to produce and permit inspection, ~~and~~ copying, testing, or sampling may, within 14 days after service of the subpoena or before the time specified for compliance if such time is less than 14 days after service, serve upon the party or attorney designated in the subpoena written objection to producing ~~inspection or copying of~~ any or all of the designated materials or inspection of the premises—or to producing electronically stored information in the form or forms requested. If objection is made, the party serving the subpoena shall not be entitled to inspect, ~~and~~ copy, test, or sample the materials or inspect the premises except pursuant to an order of the court by which the subpoena was issued. If objection has been made, the party serving the subpoena may, upon notice to the person commanded to produce, move at any time for an order to compel the production, inspection, copying, testing, or sampling. Such an order to compel ~~production~~ shall protect any person who is not a party or an officer of a party from significant expense resulting from the inspection ~~and~~, copying, testing, or sampling commanded.

(3)(A) On timely motion, the court by which a subpoena was issued shall quash or modify the subpoena if it

    (i) fails to allow reasonable time for compliance;

    (ii) requires a person who is not a party or an

officer of a party to travel to a place more than 100 miles from the place where that person resides, is employed or regularly transacts business in person, except that, subject to the provisions of clause (c)(3)(B)(iii) of this rule, such a person may in order to attend trial be commanded to travel from any such place within the state in which the trial is held; ~~or~~

(iii) requires disclosure of privileged or other protected matter and no exception or waiver applies~~;~~ or

(iv) subjects a person to undue burden.

(B) If a subpoena

(i) requires disclosure of a trade secret or other confidential research, development, or commercial information, or

(ii) requires disclosure of an unretained expert's opinion or information not describing specific events or occurrences in dispute and resulting from the expert's study made not at the request of any party, or

(iii) requires a person who is not a party or an officer of a party to incur substantial expense to travel more than 100 miles to attend trial, the court may, to protect a person subject to or affected by the subpoena, quash or modify the subpoena or, if the party in whose behalf the subpoena is issued shows a substantial need for the testimony or material that cannot be otherwise met without undue hardship and assures that the person to whom the subpoena is addressed will be reasonably compensated, the court may order appearance or production only upon specified conditions.

(d) Duties in Responding to Subpoena.

(1)(A) A person responding to a subpoena to produce documents shall produce them as they are kept in the usual course of business or shall organize and label them to correspond with the categories in the demand.

(B) If a subpoena does not specify the form or forms for producing electronically stored information, a person responding to a subpoena must produce the information in a form or forms in which the person ordinarily maintains it or in a form or forms that are reasonably usable.

(C) A person responding to a subpoena need not produce the same electronically stored information in more than one form.

(D) A person responding to a subpoena need not provide discovery of electronically stored information from sources that the person identifies as not reasonably accessible because of undue burden or cost. On motion to compel discovery or to quash, the person from whom discovery is sought must show that the information sought is not reasonably accessible because of undue burden or cost. If that showing is made, the court may nonetheless order discovery from such sources if the requesting party shows good cause, considering the limitations of Rule 26(b)(2)(C). The court may specify conditions for the discovery.

Rule 45

(2)(A) When information subject to a subpoena is withheld on a claim that it is privileged or subject to protection as trial-preparation materials, the claim shall be made expressly and shall be supported by a description of the nature of the documents, communications, or things not produced that is sufficient to enable the demanding party to contest the claim.

(B) If information is produced in response to a subpoena that is subject to a claim of privilege or of protection as trial-preparation material, the person making the claim may notify any party that received the information of the claim and the basis for it. After being notified, a party must promptly return, sequester, or destroy the specified information and any copies it has and may not use or disclose the information until the claim is resolved. A receiving party may promptly present the information to the court under seal for a determination of the claim. If the receiving party disclosed the information before being notified, it must take reasonable steps to retrieve it. The person who produced the information must preserve the information until the claim is resolved.

(e) Contempt. Failure ~~by~~ of any person without adequate excuse to obey a subpoena served upon that person may be deemed a contempt of the court from which the subpoena issued. An adequate cause for failure to obey exists when a subpoena purports to require a ~~non-party~~ nonparty to attend or produce at a place not within the limits provided by clause

Rule 45

(ii) of subparagraph (c)(3)(A).

* * * * *

Committee Note

Rule 45 is amended to conform the provisions for subpoenas to changes in other discovery rules, largely related to discovery of electronically stored information. Rule 34 is amended to provide in greater detail for the production of electronically stored information. Rule 45(a)(1)(C) is amended to recognize that electronically stored information, as defined in Rule 34(a), can also be sought by subpoena. Like Rule 34(b), Rule 45(a)(1) is amended to provide that the subpoena can designate a form or forms for production of electronic data. Rule 45(c)(2) is amended, like Rule 34(b), to authorize the person served with a subpoena to object to the requested form or forms. In addition, as under Rule 34(b), Rule 45(d)(1)(B) is amended to provide that if the subpoena does not specify the form or forms for electronically stored information, the person served with the subpoena must produce electronically stored information in a form or forms in which it is usually maintained or in a form or forms that are reasonably usable. Rule 45(d)(1)(C) is added to provide that the person producing electronically stored information should not have to produce the same information in more than one form unless so ordered by the court for good cause.

As with discovery of electronically stored information from parties, complying with a subpoena for such information may impose burdens on the responding person. Rule 45(c) provides protection against undue impositions on nonparties. For example, Rule 45(c)(1) directs that a party serving a subpoena "shall take reasonable steps to avoid imposing undue burden or expense on a person subject to the subpoena," and Rule 45(c)(2)(B) permits the person served with the subpoena to object to it and directs that an order requiring compliance "shall protect a person who is neither a party nor a party's officer from significant expense resulting from" compliance. Rule 45(d)(1)(D) is added to provide that the responding person need not provide discovery of electronically stored information from sources the party identifies as not reasonably accessible, unless the court orders such discovery for good cause, considering the limitations of Rule 26(b)(2)(C), on terms that protect a nonparty against significant expense. A parallel provision is added to Rule 26(b)(2).

Rule 45(a)(1)(B) is also amended, as is Rule 34(a), to provide that a subpoena is available to permit testing and sampling as well as inspection and copying. As in Rule 34, this change recognizes that on occasion the opportunity to perform testing or sampling may be important, both for documents and for electronically stored information. Because testing or sampling may present particular issues of burden or intrusion for the person served with the subpoena, however, the protective provisions of Rule 45(c) should be enforced with vigilance when such demands are made. Inspection or testing of certain types of electronically stored information or of a person's electronic information system may raise issues of confidentiality or privacy. The addition of sampling and testing to Rule 45(a) with regard to documents and electronically stored information is not meant to create

85

Rule 45

a routine right of direct access to a person's electronic information system, although such access might be justified in some circumstances. Courts should guard against undue intrusiveness resulting from inspecting or testing such systems.

Rule 45(d)(2) is amended, as is Rule 26(b)(5), to add a procedure for assertion of privilege or of protection as trial-preparation materials after production. The receiving party may submit the information to the court for resolution of the privilege claim, as under Rule 26(b)(5)(B).

Other minor amendments are made to conform the rule to the changes described above.

Changes Made After Publication and Comment

The Committee recommends a modified version of the proposal as published. The changes were made to maintain the parallels between Rule 45 and the other rules that address discovery of electronically stored information. These changes are fully described in the introduction to Rule 45 and in the discussions of the other rules.

The changes from the published proposed amendment are shown below.

Rule 45. Subpoena*

(a) Form; Issuance.

* * * * *

A command to produce evidence or to permit inspection, copying, testing, or sampling may be joined with a command to appear at trial or hearing or at deposition, or may be issued separately. A subpoena may specify the form or forms in which electronically stored information is to be produced.

* * * * *

(c) Protection of Persons Subject to Subpoenas.

* * * * *

(2)(B) Subject to paragraph (d)(2) of this rule, a person commanded to produce and permit inspection, copying, testing, or sampling may, within 14 days after service of

---

*Changes from the proposal published for public comment shown by double-underlining new material and striking through omitted matter.

the subpoena or before the time specified for compliance if such time is less than 14 days after service, serve upon the party or attorney designated in the subpoena written objection to providing any or all of the designated materials or <u>inspection</u> of the premises—or to providing <u>electronically stored information</u> in the form <u>or forms</u> requested. . . .

* * * * *

(d) Duties in Responding to Subpoena.

* * * * *

(B) If a subpoena does not specify the form <u>or forms</u> for producing electronically stored information, a person responding to a subpoena must produce the information in a form <u>or forms</u> in which the person ordinarily maintains it or in <u>a form or forms that are reasonably usable</u> ~~an electronically searchable form~~.

<u>**(C)**</u> The person producing electronically stored information need only produce <u>the same information</u> ~~it~~ in one form.

~~**(C)**~~<u>**(D)**</u> A person responding to a subpoena need not provide discovery of electronically stored information <u>from sources</u> that the person identifies as not reasonably accessible <u>because of undue burden or cost</u>. On motion <u>to compel discovery or to quash</u> ~~by the requesting party~~, the ~~responding party~~ <u>person from whom discovery is sought</u> must show that the information sought is not reasonably accessible <u>because of undue bur-</u>

den or cost. If that showing is made, the court may nonetheless order discovery from such sources ~~of the information for~~ if the requesting party shows good cause, considering the limitations of Rule 26(b)(2)(C). The court may specify conditions for such discovery.

(2)(A) When information subject to a subpoena is withheld on a claim that it is privileged or subject to protection as trial-preparation materials, the claim shall be made expressly and shall be supported by a description of the nature of the documents, communications, or things not produced that is sufficient to enable the demanding party to contest the claim.

(B) If ~~When a person produces~~ information is produced in response to a subpoena that is subject ~~without intending~~ to ~~waive~~ a claim of privilege or of protection as trial-preparation material, the person making the claim ~~it~~ may ~~within a reasonable time~~ notify any party that received the information of ~~its~~ the claim ~~of privilege~~ and the basis for it. After being notified, a ~~any~~ party must promptly return, sequester, or destroy the specified information and ~~all~~ any copies it has and may not disclose the information until the claim is resolved. A receiving party may promptly present the information to the court under seal for a determination of the claim. If the receiving party disclosed the information before being notified, it must take reasonable steps to retrieve it. The person who produced the information must ~~comply with Rule 45(d)(2)(A) with regard to the information and~~ preserve <u>the information until the claim is resolved</u> ~~pending a ruling by the court.~~

* * * * *

C.   CONCLUSION

When the electronic discovery proposals were published in August 2004, the Committee hoped for vigorous and broad comment from a variety of experiences and perspectives. The hearings and written comment provided many thoughtful and helpful criticisms, for which the Committee is grateful. The process has worked precisely as it should, aided by the very electronic communication capability that inspired the work in the first place.

The proposed rule amendments reflect and accommodate changes in discovery practice that have been in the making for years, brought about by profound changes in information technology. The proposed amendments work in tandem. Early attention to the issues is required. The requesting party is authorized to specify the forms in which electronically stored information should be produced and a framework is established to resolve disputes over the forms of producing such information. A party need not review or provide discovery of electronically stored information that is not reasonably accessible unless the court orders such discovery, for good cause. A procedure for asserting claims of privilege or of work-product protection after production is established. Absent exceptional circumstances, a party that is unable to provide discovery of electronically stored information lost as a result of the routine operation of an electronic information system cannot be sanctioned, if that operation was in good faith.

Electronically stored information has the potential to make discovery more efficient, less time-consuming, and less costly, if it is properly managed and effectively supervised. The volume, the dynamic character, and the numerous forms of electronically stored information, among other qualities, also have the potential to increase discovery costs and delays, further burdening the litigation process and exacerbating problems the Advisory and Standing Committees have been grappling with for years. The proposed rules provide support for early party management and, where necessary, effective judicial supervision. Keeping discovery manageable, affordable, and fair is a problem that litigants and judges in all courts share. The Committee looks forward to continuing to work to solve it fairly and well.

Rule 5(e)

[PROPOSED AMENDMENTS TO NON-DISCOVERY RELATED RULES OF CIVIL PROCEDURE]

A. Rule 5(e)

1. Discussion

The Advisory Committee recommends approval for adoption of amended Rule 5(e). The proposed amendment to Rule 5(e) authorizes adoption of local rules that require electronic filing. The proposed amendment was published last November, with parallel changes to the Appellate, Bankruptcy, and Civil Rules. The Criminal Rules incorporate the Civil Rules on filing and will absorb the proposed revision of Rule 5(e).

The published proposal was simple. It added two words to Rule 5(e), saying that a court "may by local rule permit or require" filing by electronic means. The Committee Note included this sentence: "Courts requiring electronic filing recognize the need to make exceptions for parties who cannot easily file by electronic means, and often recognize the advantage of more general 'good cause' exceptions." Several comments suggested that this Committee Note advice would not sufficiently protect litigants who face serious — perhaps insurmountable — obstacles to electronic filing. Meeting before the Civil Rules Committee, the Bankruptcy Rules Committee recommended that the parallel Bankruptcy Rule text include an express limit directing that a court reasonably accommodate parties who cannot feasibly comply with mandatory electronic filing. Several drafting alternatives were considered by the Civil Rules Committee. The Appellate Rules Committee met last, and also considered several drafting alternatives. Discussions carried on after the committee meetings led to agreement by the Appellate and Civil Rules Committees to recommend a version adding a separate sentence: "A local rule may require filing by electronic means only if reasonable exceptions are allowed."* Corresponding Committee Note language was also agreed to.

The Appellate Rules Committee proposes to include Committee Note language recognizing that a local rule may direct that a party file a hard copy of a paper that must be filed by electronic means. The Civil Rules Committee concluded that this statement is appropriate for the Appellate Rule Note because of the nearly universal desire to have paper briefs on appeal, a circumstance that distinguishes appellate practice from district court practice. District courts face a great variety of filings. At times it may be desirable to require the parties to provide hard copies of papers filed electronically, but it seems unwise

---

*The Advisory Committee had proposed language that put the rule and limit in a single sentence: ". . . may by local rule permit or — if reasonable exceptions are allowed — require papers to be filed, signed, or verified by electronic means that are consistent with technical standards, if any, that the Judicial Conference of the United States establishes." At its June 15-16, 2005, meeting, the Standing Committee adopted the separate-sentence formulation.

to attempt advice on this topic until there is more experience with mandatory electronic filing.

Rule 5. Service and Filing of Pleadings and Other Papers

* * * * *

(e) Filing with the Court Defined. The filing of papers with the court as required by these rules shall be made by filing them with the clerk of court, except that the judge may permit the papers to be filed with the judge, in which event the judge shall note thereon the filing date and forthwith transmit them to the office of the clerk. A court may by local rule permit or require papers to be filed, signed, or verified by electronic means that are consistent with technical standards, if any, that the Judicial Conference of the United States establishes. A local rule may require filing by electronic means only if reasonable exceptions are allowed. A paper filed by electronic means in compliance with a local rule constitutes a written paper for the purpose of applying these rules. The clerk shall not refuse to accept for filing any paper presented for that purpose solely because it is not presented in proper form as required by these rules or any local rules or practices.

Committee Note

Amended Rule 5(e) acknowledges that many courts have required electronic filing by means of a standing order, procedures manual, or local rule. These local practices reflect the advantages that courts and most litigants realize from electronic filing. Courts that mandate electronic filing recognize the need to make exceptions when requiring electronic filing imposes a hardship on a party. Under amended Rule 5(e), a local rule that requires electronic filing must include reasonable exceptions, but Rule 5(e) does not define the scope of those exceptions. Experience with the local rules that have been adopted and that will emerge will aid in drafting new local rules and will facilitate gradual convergence on uniform exceptions, whether in local rules or in an amended Rule 5(e).

Rule 5(e)

3. Changes Made after Publication and Comment

This recommendation is of a modified version of the proposal as published. The changes from the published version limit local rule authority to implement a caution stated in the published Committee Note. A local rule that requires electronic filing must include reasonable exceptions. This change was accomplished by a separate sentence stating that a "local rule may require filing by electronic means only if reasonable exceptions are allowed." Corresponding changes were made in the Committee Note, in collaboration with the Appellate Rules Committee. The changes from the published proposal are shown below.

Rule 5. Service and Filing of Pleadings and Other Papers*

* * * * *

(e) Filing with the Court Defined. The filing of papers with the court as required by these rules shall be made by filing them with the clerk of court, except that the judge may permit the papers to be filed with the judge, in which event the judge shall note thereon the filing date and forthwith transmit them to the office of the clerk. A court may by local rule permit or require papers to be filed, signed, or verified by electronic means that are consistent with technical standards, if any, that the Judicial Conference of the United States establishes. <u>A local rule may require filing by electronic means only if reasonable exceptions are allowed.</u> A paper filed by electronic means in compliance with a local rule constitutes a written paper for the purpose of applying these rules. The clerk shall not refuse to accept for filing any paper presented for that purpose solely because it is not presented in proper form as required by these rules or any local rules or practices.

B. Rule 50(b)

1. Discussion

---

*Changes from the proposal published for public comment shown by double-underlining new material and striking through omitted matter.

The Advisory Committee recommends approval for adoption of amended Rule 50(a) and (b). Proposed amendments of Rule 50(b) were published in August 2004. The first would permit renewal after trial of any Rule 50(a) motion for judgment as a matter of law, deleting the requirement that a motion made before the close of the evidence be renewed at the close of all the evidence. Separately, the proposed amendment adds a time limit for renewing a motion for judgment as a matter of law after the jury has failed to return a verdict on an issue addressed by the motion. Style revisions of Rule 50(a) were published at the same time.

The few comments made during the public comment period did not raise any new issues. The Committee unanimously recommends that the amendments be recommended to the Judicial Conference for adoption.

The first proposed amendment addresses the problem that arises when a party moved for judgment as a matter of law before the close of all the evidence, failed to renew the motion at the close of all the evidence, then filed a postverdict motion renewing the motion for judgment as a matter of law. The appellate decisions have begun to permit slight relaxations of the requirement that a postverdict motion be supported by — be a renewal of — a motion made at the close of all the evidence. These are departures, however, made to avoid harsh results that seemed required by the current rule language. The departures come at the price of increasingly uncertain doctrine and practice and may invite more frequent appeals. Other courts adhere to the rule's language, holding that a motion at the close of all the evidence was necessary even if the party had made an earlier motion based on the same grounds.

The proposed amendment deletes the requirement of a motion at the close of all the evidence, permitting renewal of any Rule 50(a) motion for judgment as a matter of law made during trial. The proposed amendment reflects the belief that a motion made during trial serves all the functional needs served by a motion at the close of all of the evidence. As now, the posttrial motion renews the trial motion and can be supported only by arguments made to support the trial motion. The opposing party has had clear notice of the asserted deficiencies in the case and a final opportunity to correct them. Satisfying these functional purposes equally satisfies Seventh Amendment concerns.

Separately, the proposed amendment also provides a time limit for renewing a motion for judgment as a matter of law after the jury has failed to return a verdict on an issue addressed by the motion. The Advisory Committee agenda has carried for some years the question whether to revise Rule 50(b) to establish a clear time limit for renewing a motion for judgment as a matter of law after the jury has failed to return a verdict. The question was raised by Judge Stotler while she chaired the Standing Committee. The problem appears

Rule 50(b)

on the face of the rule, which seems to allow a motion at the close of the evidence at the first trial to be renewed at any time up to ten days after judgment is entered following a second (or still later) trial. It would be folly to disregard the sufficiency of the evidence at a second trial in favor of deciding a motion based on the evidence at the first trial, and unwise to allow the question to remain open indefinitely during the period leading up to the second trial. There is authority saying that the motion must be renewed ten days after the jury is discharged. See C. Wright & A. Miller, Federal Practice & Procedure: Civil 2d, § 2357, p. 353. This authority traces to the 1938 version of Rule 50(b), which set the time for a judgment n.o.v. motion at ten days after the jury was discharged if a verdict was not returned. This provision was deleted in 1991, but the Committee Note says only that amended Rule 50(b) "retains the former requirement that a post-trial motion under the rule must be made within 10 days after entry of a contrary judgment." Research into the Advisory Committee deliberations that led to the 1991 amendment has failed to show any additional explanation. It now seems better to restore the 1991 deletion.

2. Proposed Amended Rule 50 and Committee Note

Rule 50. Judgment as a Matter of Law in Jury Trials; Alternative Motion for New Trial; Conditional Rulings

(a) Judgment as a Matter of Law.

(1) If during a trial by jury a party has been fully heard on an issue and there is no legally sufficient evidentiary basis for a reasonable jury to find for that party on that issue, the court may determine the issue against that party and may grant a motion for judgment as a matter of law against that party with respect to a claim or defense that cannot under the controlling law be maintained or defeated without a favorable finding on that issue.

(2) Motions for judgment as a matter of law may be made at any time before submission of the case to the jury. Such a motion shall specify the judgment sought and the law and the facts on which the moving party is entitled to the judgment.

(1) In General. If a party has been fully heard on an issue during a jury trial and the court finds that a reasonable

94

jury would not have a legally sufficient evidentiary basis to find for the party on that issue, the court may:

>   **(A)** resolve the issue against the party; and

>   **(B)** grant a motion for judgment as a matter of law against the party on a claim or defense that, under the controlling law, can be maintained or defeated only with a favorable finding on that issue.

>   **(2) Motion.** A motion for judgment as a matter of law may be made at any time before the case is submitted to the jury. The motion must specify the judgment sought and the law and facts that entitle the movant to the judgment.

(b) Renewing the Motion for Judgment After Trial; Alternative Motion for a New Trial. If, for any reason, the court does not grant a motion for judgment as a matter of law made at the close of all the evidence under subdivision (a), the court is considered to have submitted the action to the jury subject to the court's later deciding the legal questions raised by the motion. The movant may renew its request for judgment as a matter of law by filing a motion no later than 10 days after the entry of judgment or—if the motion addresses a jury issue not decided by a verdict—no later than 10 days after the jury was discharged. — and The movant may alternatively request a new trial or join a motion for a new trial under Rule 59.

In ruling on a renewed motion, the court may:

>   **(1)** if a verdict was returned:

>>   **(A)** allow the judgment to stand,

>>   **(B)** order a new trial, or

>>   **(C)** direct entry of judgment as a matter of law; or

Rule 50(b)

(2) if no verdict was returned:

(A) order a new trial, or

(B) direct entry of judgment as a matter of law.

* * * * *

Committee Note

The language of Rule 50(a) has been amended as part of the general restyling of the Civil Rules to make them more easily understood and to make style and terminology consistent throughout the rules. These changes are intended to be stylistic only.

Rule 50(b) is amended to permit renewal of any Rule 50(a) motion for judgment as a matter of law, deleting the requirement that a motion be made at the close of all the evidence. Because the Rule 50(b) motion is only a renewal of the preverdict motion, it can be granted only on grounds advanced in the preverdict motion. The earlier motion informs the opposing party of the challenge to the sufficiency of the evidence and affords a clear opportunity to provide additional evidence that may be available. The earlier motion also alerts the court to the opportunity to simplify the trial by resolving some issues, or even all issues, without submission to the jury. This fulfillment of the functional needs that underlie present Rule 50(b) also satisfies the Seventh Amendment. Automatic reservation of the legal questions raised by the motion conforms to the decision in Baltimore & Carolina Line v. Redman, 297 U.S. 654 (1935).

This change responds to many decisions that have begun to move away from requiring a motion for judgment as a matter of law at the literal close of all the evidence. Although the requirement has been clearly established for several decades, lawyers continue to overlook it. The courts are slowly working away from the formal requirement. The amendment establishes the functional approach that courts have been unable to reach under the present rule and makes practice more consistent and predictable.

Many judges expressly invite motions at the close of all the evidence. The amendment is not intended to discourage this useful practice.

Finally, an explicit time limit is added for making a posttrial motion when the trial ends without a verdict or with a verdict that does not dispose of all issues suitable for resolution by verdict. The motion must be made no later than 10 days after the jury was discharged.

3. Changes Made After Publication and Comment

This recommendation modifies the version of the proposal as published. The only changes made in the rule text after publication are matters of style. One sentence in the Committee Note was changed by adopting the wording of the 1991 Committee Note describing the grounds that may be used to support a renewed motion for judgment as a matter of law. A paragraph also was added to the Committee Note to explain the style revisions in subdivision (a). The changes from the published rule text are set out below.

Rule 50. Judgment as a Matter of Law in Jury Trials; Alternative Motion for New Trial; Conditional Rulings*

(a) Judgment as a Matter of Law.

* * * * *

(1) In General. If a party has been fully heard on an issue during a jury trial and the court finds that a reasonable jury would not have a legally sufficient evidentiary basis to find for the party on that issue, the court may:

(A) ~~determine~~ <u>resolve</u> the issue against the party; and

* * * * *

(b) Renewing the Motion After Trial; Alternative Motion for a New Trial. If the court does not grant a motion for judgment as a matter of law made under subdivision (a), the court is ~~deemed~~ <u>considered</u> to have submitted the action to the jury subject to the court's later deciding the legal questions raised by the motion.

* * * * *

(4) Supplemental Rule G, with Conforming Changes To Supplemental Rules A, C, E and Civil Rules 9, 14, and 65.1; and Rule 26(a)(1)(E)

Admiralty Rule G: Civil Forfeiture

Admiralty Rule G represents the culmination of several years of work to adapt the Supplemental Rules to the great growth of civil forfeiture actions. Many civil forfeiture statutes explicitly invoke the Supplemental Rules. The procedures that best serve civil forfeiture actions, however, often depart from the procedures that best serve traditional admiralty and maritime actions. Rule G was developed in close cooperation with the Department of Justice and representatives of the National Association of Criminal Defense Lawyers to establish distinctive forfeiture procedures within the framework of the Supplemental Rules. In addition, Rule G establishes new provisions to reflect enactment of the Civil Asset Forfeiture Reform Act of 2000, and to reflect developments

---

*Changes from the proposal published for public comment shown by double-underlining new material and striking through omitted matter.

Supplemental Rule G

in decisional and constitutional law. The result is a nearly complete separation of civil forfeiture procedure from Supplemental Rules A through F, invoking them for civil forfeiture only to address interstitial questions that are not covered by Rule G.

The only lengthy comments on Rule G were provided by the Department of Justice. A summary of all the comments is set out below.

Several modest changes in Rule G and the Committee Note are proposed as a result of the comments.

Conforming amendments to other Supplemental Rules were published with Rule G. An addition to Rule 26(a)(1)(E) was published, adding "a forfeiture action in rem arising from a federal statute" to the exemptions from initial disclosure requirements. There was no comment on these amendments.

In addition to the published proposals, technical changes are needed to conform Rule 9(h) to the new Rule G title and to conform Rule 14 cross-references to the Supplemental Rule C(6) provisions redesignated in the conforming amendments that were published with Rule G. Because these changes are purely mechanical, they are recommended for adoption without publication.

With the changes proposed below, it is recommended that Rule G be sent to the Judicial Conference with a recommendation for adoption.

SUPPLEMENTAL RULES FOR ~~CERTAIN~~ ADMIRALTY ~~AND~~ OR MARITIME <u>CLAIMS AND ASSET FORFEITURE</u> ~~CLAIMS~~ <u>ACTIONS</u>

<u>Rule G. Forfeiture Actions In Rem</u>

<u>(1) Scope.</u> <u>This rule governs a forfeiture action in rem arising from a federal statute. To the extent that this rule does not address an issue, Supplemental Rules C and E and the Federal Rules of Civil Procedure also apply.</u>

<u>(2) Complaint.</u> <u>The complaint must:</u>

<u>(a) be verified;</u>

<u>(b) state the grounds for subject-matter jurisdiction, in rem jurisdiction over the defendant property, and venue;</u>

<u>(c) describe the property with reasonable particularity;</u>

(d) if the property is tangible, state its location when any seizure occurred and — if different — its location when the action is filed;

(e) identify the statute under which the forfeiture action is brought; and

(f) state sufficiently detailed facts to support a reasonable belief that the government will be able to meet its burden of proof at trial.

(3) Judicial Authorization and Process.

(a) Real Property. If the defendant is real property, the government must proceed under 18 U. S. C. § 985.

(b) Other Property; Arrest Warrant. If the defendant is not real property:

(i) the clerk must issue a warrant to arrest the property if it is in the government's possession, custody, or control;

(ii) the court — on finding probable cause — must issue a warrant to arrest the property if it is not in the government's possession, custody, or control and is not subject to a judicial restraining order; and

(iii) a warrant is not necessary if the property is subject to a judicial restraining order.

(c) Execution of Process.

(i) The warrant and any supplemental process must be delivered to a person or organization authorized to execute it, who may be: (A) a marshal or any other United States officer or employee; (B) someone under contract with the United States; or

(C) someone specially appointed by the court for that purpose.

 (ii) The authorized person or organization must execute the warrant and any supplemental process on property in the United States as soon as practicable unless:

(A) the property is in the government's possession, custody, or control; or

(B) the court orders a different time when the complaint is under seal, the action is stayed before the warrant and supplemental process are executed, or the court finds other good cause.

(iii) The warrant and any supplemental process may be executed within the district or, when authorized by statute, outside the district.

(iv) If executing a warrant on property outside the United States is required, the warrant may be transmitted to an appropriate authority for serving process where the property is located.

(4) Notice.

(a) Notice by Publication.

(i) When Publication Is Required. A judgment of forfeiture may be entered only if the government has published notice of the action within a reasonable time after filing the complaint or at a time the court orders. But notice need not be published if:

(A) the defendant property is worth less than $1,000 and direct notice is sent under Rule

G(4)(b) to every person the government can reasonably identify as a potential claimant; or

(B) the court finds that the cost of publication exceeds the property's value and that other means of notice would satisfy due process.

(ii) Content of the Notice. Unless the court orders otherwise, the notice must:

(A) describe the property with reasonable particularity;

(B) state the times under Rule G(5) to file a claim and to answer; and

(C) name the government attorney to be served with the claim and answer.

(iii) Frequency of Publication. Published notice must appear:

(A) once a week for three consecutive weeks; or

(B) only once if, before the action was filed, notice of nonjudicial forfeiture of the same property was published on an official internet government forfeiture site for at least 30 consecutive days, or in a newspaper of general circulation for three consecutive weeks in a district where publication is authorized under Rule G(4)(a)(iv).

(iv) Means of Publication. The government should select from the following options a means of publication reasonably calculated to notify potential claimants of the action:

(A) if the property is in the United States, publication in a newspaper generally circulated in the district where the action is filed, where the property was seized, or where property that was not seized is located;

(B) if the property is outside the United States, publication in a newspaper generally circulated in a district where the action is filed, in a newspaper generally circulated in the country where the property is located, or in legal notices published and generally circulated in the country where the property is located; or

(C) instead of (A) or (B), posting a notice on an official internet government forfeiture site for at least 30 consecutive days.

(b) Notice to Known Potential Claimants.

(i) Direct Notice Required. The government must send notice of the action and a copy of the complaint to any person who reasonably appears to be a potential claimant on the facts known to the government before the end of the time for filing a claim under Rule G(5)(a)(ii)(B).

(ii) Content of the Notice. The notice must state:

(A) the date when the notice is sent;

(B) a deadline for filing a claim, at least 35 days after the notice is sent;

(C) that an answer or a motion under Rule

12 must be filed no later than 20 days after filing the claim; and

(D) the name of the government attorney to be served with the claim and answer.

(iii) Sending Notice.

(A) The notice must be sent by means reasonably calculated to reach the potential claimant.

(B) Notice may be sent to the potential claimant or to the attorney representing the potential claimant with respect to the seizure of the property or in a related investigation, administrative forfeiture proceeding, or criminal case.

(C) Notice sent to a potential claimant who is incarcerated must be sent to the place of incarceration.

(D) Notice to a person arrested in connection with an offense giving rise to the forfeiture who is not incarcerated when notice is sent may be sent to the address that person last gave to the agency that arrested or released the person.

(E) Notice to a person from whom the property was seized who is not incarcerated when notice is sent may be sent to the last address that person gave to the agency that seized the property.

(iv) When Notice Is Sent.
Notice by the following means is sent on the date when it is placed in the mail, delivered to a commercial carrier, or sent by electronic mail.

(v) Actual Notice. A potential claimant who had actual notice of a forfeiture action may not oppose or seek relief from forfeiture because of the government's failure to send the required notice.

(5) Responsive Pleadings.

(a) Filing a Claim.

(i) A person who asserts an interest in the defendant property may contest the forfeiture by filing a claim in the court where the action is pending. The claim must:

(A) identify the specific property claimed;

(B) identify the claimant and state the claimant's interest in the property;

(C) be signed by the claimant under penalty of perjury; and

(D) be served on the government attorney designated under Rule G(4)(a)(ii)(C) or (b)(ii)(D).

(ii) Unless the court for good cause sets a different time, the claim must be filed:

(A) by the time stated in a direct notice sent under Rule G(4)(b);

(B) if notice was published but direct notice was not sent to the claimant or the claimant's attorney, no later than 30 days after final publication of newspaper notice or legal notice under Rule G(4)(a) or no later than 60 days after the first day of publication on an official internet government forfeiture site; or

(C) if notice was not published and direct notice was not sent to the claimant or the claimant's attorney:

(1) if the property was in the government's possession, custody, or control when the complaint was filed, no later than 60 days after the filing, not counting any time when the complaint was under seal or when the action was stayed before execution of a warrant issued under Rule G(3)(b); or

(2) if the property was not in the government's possession, custody, or control when the complaint was filed, no later than 60 days after the government complied with 18 U.S.C. § 985(c) as to real property, or 60 days after process was executed on the property under Rule G(3).

(iii) A claim filed by a person asserting an interest as a bailee must identify the bailor, and if filed on the bailor's behalf must state the authority to do so.

(b) Answer. A claimant must serve and file an answer to the complaint or a motion under Rule 12 within 20 days after filing the claim. A claimant waives an objection to in rem jurisdiction or to venue if the objection is not made by motion or stated in the answer.

(6) Special Interrogatories.

(a) Time and Scope. The government may serve special interrogatories limited to the claimant's identity and relationship to the defendant property without the court's leave at any time after the claim is filed and before discovery is closed. But if the claimant serves a motion to dismiss the action, the government must serve the interrogatories within 20 days after the motion is served.

(b) Answers or Objections. Answers or objections to these interrogatories must be served within 20 days after the interrogatories are served.

(c) Government's Response Deferred. The government need not respond to a claimant's motion to dismiss the action under Rule G(8)(b) until 20 days after the claimant has answered these interrogatories.

(7) Preserving, Preventing Criminal Use, and Disposing of Property; Sales.

(a) Preserving and Preventing Criminal Use of Property. When the government does not have actual possession of the defendant property the court, on motion or on its own, may enter any order necessary to preserve the property, to prevent its removal or encumbrance, or to prevent its use in a criminal offense.

(b) Interlocutory Sale or Delivery.

(i) Order to Sell. On motion by a party or a person having custody of the property, the court may order all or part of the property sold if:

(A) the property is perishable or at risk of deterioration, decay, or injury by being detained in custody pending the action;

(B) the expense of keeping the property is excessive or is disproportionate to its fair market value;

(C) the property is subject to a mortgage or to

taxes on which the owner is in default; or

(D) the court finds other good cause.

(ii) **Who Makes the Sale.** A sale must be made by a United States agency that has authority to sell the property, by the agency's contractor, or by any person the court designates.

(iii) **Sale Procedures.** The sale is governed by 28 U.S.C. §§ 2001, 2002, and 2004, unless all parties, with the court's approval, agree to the sale, aspects of the sale, or different procedures.

(iv) **Sale Proceeds.** Sale proceeds are a substitute res subject to forfeiture in place of the property that was sold. The proceeds must be held in an interest-bearing account maintained by the United States pending the conclusion of the forfeiture action.

(v) **Delivery on a Claimant's Motion.** The court may order that the property be delivered to the claimant pending the conclusion of the action if the claimant shows circumstances that would permit sale under Rule G(7)(b)(i) and gives security under these rules.

(c) **Disposing of Forfeited Property.** Upon entry of a forfeiture judgment, the property or proceeds from selling the property must be disposed of as provided by law.

(8) **Motions.**

(a) **Motion To Suppress Use of the Property as Evidence.** If the defendant property was seized, a party with standing to contest the lawfulness of the seizure may move to suppress use of the property as evidence. Suppression does not affect forfeiture of the property based on independently derived evidence.

(b) Motion To Dismiss the Action.

(i) A claimant who establishes standing to contest forfeiture may move to dismiss the action under Rule 12(b).

(ii) In an action governed by 18 U.S.C. § 983(a)(3)(D) the complaint may not be dismissed on the ground that the government did not have adequate evidence at the time the complaint was filed to establish the forfeitability of the property. The sufficiency of the complaint is governed by Rule G(2).

(c) Motion To Strike a Claim or Answer.

(i) At any time before trial, the government may move to strike a claim or answer:

(A) for failing to comply with Rule G(5) or (6);, or

(B) because the claimant lacks standing.

(ii) The motion:

(A) must be decided before any motion by the claimant to dismiss the action; and

(B) may be presented as a motion for judgment on the pleadings or as a motion to determine after a hearing or by summary judgment whether the claimant can carry the burden of establishing standing by a preponderance of the evidence.

(d) Petition To Release Property.

(i) If a United States agency or an agency's contractor holds property for judicial or nonjudicial forfeiture under a statute governed by 18 U.S.C. § 983(f), a person who has filed a claim to the property may petition for its release under § 983(f).

(ii) If a petition for release is filed before a judicial forfeiture action is filed against the property, the petition may be filed either in the district where the property was seized or in the district where a warrant to seize the property issued. If a judicial forfeiture action against the property is later filed in another district — or if the government shows that the action will be filed in another district — the petition may be transferred to that district under 28 U.S.C. § 1404.

(e) Excessive Fines. A claimant may seek to mitigate a forfeiture under the Excessive Fines Clause of the Eighth Amendment by motion for summary judgment or by motion made after entry of a forfeiture judgment if:

(i) the claimant has pleaded the defense under Rule 8; and

(ii) the parties have had the opportunity to conduct civil discovery on the defense.

(9) Trial. Trial is to the court unless any party demands trial by jury under Rule 38.

Committee Note

Rule G is added to bring together the central procedures that govern civil forfeiture actions. Civil forfeiture actions are in rem proceedings, as are many admiralty proceedings. As the number of civil forfeiture actions has increased, however, reasons have appeared to create sharper distinctions within the framework of the Supplemental Rules. Civil forfeiture practice will benefit from distinctive provisions that express and focus developments in statutory, constitutional, and decisional law. Admiralty practice will be freed from the pressures that arise when the needs of civil

Supplemental Rule G

forfeiture proceedings counsel interpretations of common rules that may not be suitable for admiralty proceedings.

Rule G generally applies to actions governed by the Civil Asset Forfeiture Reform Act of 2000 (CAFRA) and also to actions excluded from it. The rule refers to some specific CAFRA provisions; if these statutes are amended, the rule should be adapted to the new provisions during the period required to amend the rule.

Rule G is not completely self-contained. Subdivision (1) recognizes the need to rely at times on other Supplemental Rules and the place of the Supplemental Rules within the basic framework of the Civil Rules.

Supplemental Rules A, C, and E are amended to reflect the adoption of Rule G.

Subdivision (1)

Rule G is designed to include the distinctive procedures that govern a civil forfeiture action. Some details, however, are better supplied by relying on Rules C and E. Subdivision (1) incorporates those rules for issues not addressed by Rule G. This general incorporation is at times made explicit — subdivision (7)(b)(v), for example, invokes the security provisions of Rule E. But Rules C and E are not to be invoked to create conflicts with Rule G. They are to be used only when Rule G, fairly construed, does not address the issue.

The Civil Rules continue to provide the procedural framework within which Rule G and the other Supplemental Rules operate. Both Rule G(1) and Rule A state this basic proposition. Rule G, for example, does not address pleadings amendments. Civil Rule 15 applies, in light of the circumstances of a forfeiture action.

Subdivision (2)

Rule E(2)(a) requires that the complaint in an admiralty action "state the circumstances from which the claim arises with such particularity that the defendant or claimant will be able, without moving for a more definite statement, to commence an investigation of the facts and to frame a responsive pleading." Application of this standard to civil forfeiture actions has evolved to the standard stated in subdivision (2)(f). The complaint must state sufficiently detailed facts to support a reasonable belief that the government will be able to meet its burden of proof at trial. See U. S. v. Mondragon, 313 F.3d 862 (4th Cir. 2002). Subdivision (2)(f) carries this forfeiture case law forward without change.

Subdivision (3)

Subdivision (3) governs in rem process in a civil forfeiture action.

Paragraph (a). Paragraph (a) reflects the provisions of 18 U.S.C. § 985.

Paragraph (b). Paragraph (b) addresses arrest warrants when the defendant is not real property. Subparagraph (i) directs the clerk to issue a warrant if the property is in the government's possession, custody, or control.

If the property is not in the government's possession, custody, or control and is not subject to a restraining order, subparagraph (ii) provides that a warrant issues only if the court finds probable cause to arrest the property. This provision departs from former Rule C(3)(a)(i), which authorized issuance of summons and warrant by the clerk without a probable-cause finding. The probable-cause finding better protects the interests of persons interested in the property. Subparagraph (iii) recognizes that a warrant is not necessary if the property is subject to a judicial restraining order. The government remains free, however, to seek a warrant if it anticipates that the restraining order may be modified or vacated.

Paragraph (c). Subparagraph (ii) requires that the warrant and any supplemental process be served as soon as practicable unless the property is already in the government's possession, custody, or control. But it authorizes the court to order a different time. The authority to order a different time recognizes that the government may have secured orders sealing the complaint in a civil forfeiture action or have won a stay after filing. The seal or stay may be ordered for reasons, such as protection of an ongoing criminal investigation, that would be defeated by prompt service of the warrant. Subparagraph (ii) does not reflect any independent ground for ordering a seal or stay, but merely reflects the consequences for execution when sealing or a stay is ordered. A court also may order a different time for service if good cause is shown for reasons unrelated to a seal or stay. Subparagraph (iv) reflects the uncertainty surrounding service of an arrest warrant on property not in the United States. It is not possible to identify in the rule the appropriate authority for serving process in all other countries. Transmission of the warrant to an appropriate authority, moreover, does not ensure that the warrant will be executed. The rule requires only that the warrant be transmitted to an appropriate authority.

Subdivision (4)

Paragraph (a). Paragraph (a) reflects the traditional practice of publishing notice of an in rem action.

Subparagraph (i) recognizes two exceptions to the general publication requirement. Publication is not required if the defendant property is worth less than $1,000 and direct notice is sent to all reasonably identifiable potential claimants as required by subdivision (4)(b). Publication also is not required if the cost would exceed the property's value and the court finds that other means of notice would satisfy due process. Publication on a government-established internet forfeiture site, as contemplated by subparagraph (iv), would be at a low marginal publication cost, which would likely be the cost to compare to the property value.

Subparagraph (iv) states the basic criterion for selecting the means and method of publication. The purpose is to adopt a means reasonably calculated to reach potential claimants. The government should choose from among these means a method that is reasonably likely to reach potential claimants at a cost reasonable in the circumstances.

If the property is in the United States and newspaper notice is chosen, publication may be where the action is filed, where the property was seized, or — if the property was not seized — where the property is located. Choice among these places is influenced by the probable location of potential claimants.

If the property is not in the United States, account must be taken of the sensitivities that surround publication of legal notices in other countries. A foreign country may forbid local publication. If potential claimants are likely to be in the United States, publication in the district where the action is filed may be the best choice. If potential claimants are likely to be located abroad, the better choice may be publication by means generally circulated in the country where the property is located.

Newspaper publication is not a particularly effective means of notice for most potential claimants. Its traditional use is best defended by want of affordable alternatives. Paragraph (iv)(C) contemplates a government-created internet forfeiture site that would provide a single easily identified means of notice. Such a site could allow much more direct access to notice as to any specific property than publication provides.

Paragraph (b). Paragraph (b) is entirely new. For the first time, Rule G expressly recognizes the due process obligation to send notice to any person who reasonably appears to be a potential claimant.

Subparagraph (i) states the obligation to send notice. Many potential claimants will be known to the government because they have filed claims during the administrative forfeiture stage. Notice must be sent, however, no matter what source of information makes it reasonably appear that a person is a potential claimant. The duty to send notice terminates when the time for filing a claim expires.

Notice of the action does not require formal service of summons in the manner required by Rule 4 to initiate a personal action. The process that begins an in rem forfeiture action is addressed by subdivision (3). This process commonly gives notice to potential claimants. Publication of notice is required in addition to this process. Due process requirements have moved beyond these traditional means of notice, but are satisfied by practical means that are reasonably calculated to accomplish actual notice.

Subparagraph (ii)(B) directs that the notice state a deadline for filing a claim that is at least 35 days after the notice is sent. This provision applies both in actions that fall within 18 U.S.C.

§ 983(a)(4)(A) and in other actions. Section 983(a)(4)(A) states that a claim should be filed no later than 30 days after service of the complaint. The variation introduced by subparagraph (ii)(B) reflects the procedure of § 983(a)(2)(B) for nonjudicial forfeiture proceedings. The nonjudicial procedure requires that a claim be filed "not later than the deadline set forth in a personal notice letter (which may be not earlier than 35 days after the date the letter is sent) * * *." This procedure is as suitable in a civil forfeiture action as in a nonjudicial forfeiture proceeding. Thirty-five days after notice is sent ordinarily will extend the claim time by no more than a brief period; a claimant anxious to expedite proceedings can file the claim before the deadline; and the government has flexibility to set a still longer period when circumstances make that desirable.

Subparagraph (iii) begins by stating the basic requirement that notice must be sent by means reasonably calculated to reach the potential claimant. No attempt is made to list the various means that may be reasonable in different circumstances. It may be reasonable, for example, to rely on means that have already been established for communication with a particular potential claimant. The government's interest in choosing a means likely to accomplish actual notice is bolstered by its desire to avoid post-forfeiture challenges based on arguments that a different method would have been more likely to accomplish actual notice. Flexible rule language accommodates the rapid evolution of communications technology.

Notice may be directed to a potential claimant through counsel, but only to counsel already representing the claimant with respect to the seizure of the property, or in a related investigation, administrative forfeiture proceeding, or criminal case.

Subparagraph (iii)(C) reflects the basic proposition that notice to a potential claimant who is incarcerated must be sent to the place of incarceration. Notice directed to some other place, such as a pre-incarceration residence, is less likely to reach the potential claimant. This provision does not address due process questions that may arise if a particular prison has deficient procedures for delivering notice to prisoners. See Dusenbery v. U.S., 534 U.S. 161 (2002).

Items (D) and (E) of subparagraph (iii) authorize the government to rely on an address given by a person who is not incarcerated. The address may have been given to the agency that arrested or released the person, or to the agency that seized the property. The government is not obliged to undertake an independent investigation to verify the address.

Subparagraph (iv) identifies the date on which notice is considered to be sent for some common means, without addressing the circumstances for choosing among the identified means or other means. The date of sending should be determined by analogy for means not listed. Facsimile transmission, for example, is sent upon transmission. Notice by personal delivery is sent on delivery.

Subparagraph (v), finally, reflects the purpose to effect actual notice by providing that a potential claimant who had actual notice of a forfeiture proceeding cannot oppose or seek relief from forfeiture because the government failed to comply with subdivision (4)(b).

Subdivision (5)

Paragraph (a). Paragraph (a) establishes that the first step of contesting a civil forfeiture action is to file a claim. A claim is required by 18 U.S.C. § 983(a)(4)(A) for actions covered by § 983. Paragraph (a) applies this procedure as well to actions not covered by § 983. "Claim" is used to describe this first pleading because of the statutory references to claim and claimant. It functions in the same way as the statement of interest prescribed for an admiralty proceeding by Rule C(6), and is not related to the distinctive meaning of "claim" in admiralty practice.

If the claimant states its interest in the property to be as bailee, the bailor must be identified. A bailee who files a claim on behalf of a bailor must state the bailee's authority to do so.

The claim must be signed under penalty of perjury by the person making it. An artificial body that can act only through an agent may authorize an agent to sign for it. Excusable inability of counsel to obtain an appropriate signature may be grounds for an extension of time to file the claim.

Paragraph (a)(ii) sets the time for filing a claim. Item (C) applies in the relatively rare circumstance in which notice is not published and the government did not send direct notice to the claimant because it did not know of the claimant or did not have an address for the claimant.

Paragraph (b). Under 18 U.S.C. § 983(a)(4)(B), which governs many forfeiture proceedings, a person who asserts an interest by filing a claim "shall file an answer to the Government's complaint for forfeiture not later than 20 days after the date of the filing of the claim." Paragraph (b) recognizes that this statute works within the general procedures established by Civil Rule 12. Rule 12(a)(4) suspends the time to answer when a Rule 12 motion is served within the time allowed to answer. Continued application of this rule to proceedings governed by § 983(a)(4)(B) serves all of the purposes advanced by Rule 12(a)(4), see U.S. v. $8,221,877.16, 330 F.3d 141 (3d Cir. 2003); permits a uniform procedure for all civil forfeiture actions; and recognizes that a motion under Rule 12 can be made only after a claim is filed that provides background for the motion.

Failure to present an objection to in rem jurisdiction or to venue by timely motion or answer waives the objection. Waiver of such objections is familiar. An answer may be amended to assert an objection initially omitted. But Civil Rule 15 should be applied to an amendment that for the first time raises an objection to in rem jurisdiction by analogy to the personal jurisdiction objection provision in Civil Rule 12(h)(1)(B). The amendment should be permitted only if it is permitted as a matter of course under Rule 15(a).

A claimant's motion to dismiss the action is further governed by subdivisions (6)(c), (8)(b), and (8)(c).

Subdivision (6)

Subdivision (6) illustrates the adaptation of an admiralty procedure to the different needs of civil forfeiture. Rule C(6) permits interrogatories to be served with the complaint in an in rem action without limiting the subjects of inquiry. Civil forfeiture practice does not require such an extensive departure from ordinary civil practice. It remains useful, however, to permit the government to file limited interrogatories at any time after a claim is filed to gather information that bears on the claimant's standing. Subdivisions (8)(b) and (c) allow a claimant to move to dismiss only if the claimant has standing, and recognize the government's right to move to dismiss a claim for lack of standing. Subdivision (6) interrogatories are integrated with these provisions in that the interrogatories are limited to the claimant's identity and relationship to the defendant property. If the claimant asserts a relationship to the property as bailee, the interrogatories can inquire into the bailor's interest in the property and the bailee's relationship to the bailor. The claimant can accelerate the time to serve subdivision (6) interrogatories by serving a motion to dismiss — the interrogatories must be served within 20 days after the motion is served. Integration is further accomplished by deferring the government's obligation to respond to a motion to dismiss until 20 days after the claimant moving to dismiss has answered the interrogatories.

Special interrogatories served under Rule G(6) do not count against the presumptive 25-interrogatory limit established by Rule 33(a). Rule 33 procedure otherwise applies to these interrogatories.

Subdivision (6) supersedes the discovery "moratorium" of Rule 26(d) and the broader interrogatories permitted for admiralty proceedings by Rule C(6).

Subdivision (7)

Paragraph (a). Paragraph (a) is adapted from Rule E(9)(b). It provides for preservation orders when the government does not have actual possession of the defendant property. It also goes beyond Rule E(9) by recognizing the need to prevent use of the defendant property in ongoing criminal offenses.

Paragraph (b). Paragraph (b)(i)(C) recognizes the authority, already exercised in some cases, to order sale of property subject to a defaulted mortgage or to defaulted taxes. The authority is narrowly confined to mortgages and tax liens; other lien interests may be addressed, if at all, only through the general good-cause provision. The court must carefully weigh the competing interests in each case.

Paragraph (b)(i)(D) establishes authority to order sale for good cause. Good cause may be shown when the property is subject to diminution in value. Care should be taken before ordering sale to avoid diminished value.

Paragraph (b)(iii) recognizes that if the court approves, the interests of all parties may be served by their agreement to sale, aspects of the sale, or sale procedures that depart from governing statutory procedures.

Paragraph (c) draws from Rule E(9)(a), (b), and (c). Disposition of the proceeds as provided by law may require resolution of disputed issues. A mortgagee's claim to the property or sale proceeds, for example, may be disputed on the ground that the mortgage is not genuine. An undisputed lien claim, on the other hand, may be recognized by payment after an interlocutory sale.

Subdivision (8)

Subdivision (8) addresses a number of issues that are unique to civil forfeiture actions.

Supplemental Rule G

Paragraph (a). Standing to suppress use of seized property as evidence is governed by principles distinct from the principles that govern claim standing. A claimant with standing to contest forfeiture may not have standing to seek suppression. Rule G does not of itself create a basis of suppression standing that does not otherwise exist.

Paragraph (b). Paragraph (b)(i) is one element of the system that integrates the procedures for determining a claimant's standing to claim and for deciding a claimant's motion to dismiss the action. Under paragraph (c)(ii), a motion to dismiss the action cannot be addressed until the court has decided any government motion to strike the claim or answer. This procedure is reflected in the (b)(i) reminder that a motion to dismiss the forfeiture action may be made only by a claimant who establishes claim standing. The government, moreover, need not respond to a claimant's motion to dismiss until 20 days after the claimant has answered any subdivision (6) interrogatories.

Paragraph (b)(ii) mirrors 18 U.S.C. § 983(a)(3)(D). It applies only to an action independently governed by § 983(a)(3)(D), implying nothing as to actions outside § 983(a)(3)(D). The adequacy of the complaint is measured against the pleading requirements of subdivision (2), not against the quality of the evidence available to the government when the complaint was filed.

Paragraph (c). As noted with paragraph (b), paragraph (c) governs the procedure for determining whether a claimant has standing. It does not address the principles that govern claim standing.

Paragraph (c)(i)(A) provides that the government may move to strike a claim or answer for failure to comply with the pleading requirements of subdivision (5) or to answer subdivision (6) interrogatories. As with other pleadings, the court should strike a claim or answer only if satisfied that an opportunity should not be afforded to cure the defects under Rule 15. Not every failure to respond to subdivision (6) interrogatories warrants an order striking the claim. But the special role that subdivision (6) plays in the scheme for determining claim standing may justify a somewhat more demanding approach than the general approach to discovery sanctions under Rule 37.

Paragraph (c)(ii) directs that a motion to strike a claim or answer be decided before any motion by the claimant to dismiss the action. A claimant who lacks standing is not entitled to challenge the forfeiture on the merits.

Paragraph (c)(ii) further identifies three procedures for addressing claim standing. If a claim fails on its face to show facts that support claim standing, the claim can be dismissed by judgment on the pleadings. If the claim shows facts that would support claim standing, those facts can be tested by a motion for summary judgment. If material facts are disputed, precluding a grant of summary judgment, the court may hold an evidentiary hearing. The evidentiary hearing is held by the court without a jury. The claimant has the burden to establish claim standing at a hearing; procedure on a government summary judgment motion reflects this allocation of the burden.

Paragraph (d). The hardship release provisions of 18 U.S.C. § 983(f) do not apply to a civil forfeiture action exempted from § 983 by § 983(i).

Paragraph (d)(ii) reflects the venue provisions of 18 U.S.C. § 983(f)(3)(A) as a guide to practitioners. In addition, it makes clear the status of a civil forfeiture action as a "civil action" eligible for transfer under 28 U.S.C. § 1404. A transfer decision must be made on the circumstances of the particular proceeding. The district where the forfeiture action is filed has the advantage of bringing all related proceedings together, avoiding the waste that flows from consideration of different parts of the same forfeiture proceeding in the court where the warrant issued or the court where the property was seized. Transfer to that court would serve consolidation, the purpose that underlies nationwide enforcement of a seizure warrant. But there may be offsetting advantages in retaining the petition where it was filed. The claimant may not be able to litigate, effectively or at all, in a distant court. Issues relevant to the petition may be better litigated where the property was seized or where the warrant issued. One element, for example, is whether the claimant has sufficient ties to the community to provide assurance that the property will be available at the time of trial. Another is whether continued government possession would prevent the claimant from working. Determining whether seizure of the claimant's automobile prevents work may turn on assessing the realities of local public transit facilities.

Paragraph (e). The Excessive Fines Clause of the Eighth Amendment forbids an excessive forfeiture. U.S. v. Bajakajian, 524 U.S. 321 (1998). 18 U.S.C. § 983(g) provides a "petition" "to determine whether the forfeiture was constitutionally excessive" based on finding "that the forfeiture is grossly disproportional to the offense." Paragraph (e) describes the procedure for § 983(g) mitigation petitions and adopts the same procedure for forfeiture actions that fall outside § 983(g). The procedure is by motion, either for summary judgment or for mitigation after a forfeiture judgment is entered. The claimant must give notice of this defense by pleading, but failure to raise the defense in the initial answer may be cured by amendment under Rule 15. The issues that bear on mitigation often are separate from the issues that determine forfeiture. For that reason it may be convenient to resolve the issue by summary judgment before trial on the forfeiture issues. Often, however, it will be more convenient to determine first whether the property is to be forfeited. Whichever time is chosen to address mitigation, the parties must have had the opportunity to conduct civil discovery on the defense. The extent and timing of discovery are governed by the ordinary rules.

Subdivision (9)

Subdivision (9) serves as a reminder of the need to demand jury trial under Rule 38. It does not expand the right to jury trial. See U.S. v. One Parcel of Property Located at 32 Medley Lane, 2005 WL 465241 (D.Conn.2005), ruling that the court, not the jury, determines whether a forfeiture is constitutionally excessive.

Supplemental Rule G

Changes Made After Publication and Comment

Rule G(6)(a) was amended to delete the provision that special interrogatories addressed to a claimant's standing are "under Rule 33." The government was concerned that some forfeitures raise factually complex standing issues that require many interrogatories, severely depleting the presumptive 25-interrogatory limit in Rule 33. The Committee Note is amended to state that the interrogatories do not count against the limit, but that Rule 33 governs the procedure.

Rule G(7)(a) was amended to recognize the court's authority to enter an order necessary to prevent use of the defendant property in a criminal offense.

Rule G(8)(c) was revised to clarify the use of three procedures to challenge a claimant's standing — judgment on the pleadings, summary judgment, or an evidentiary hearing.

Several other rule text changes were made to add clarity on small points or to conform to Style conventions.

Changes were made in the Committee Note to explain some of the rule text revisions, to add clarity on a few points, and to delete statements about complex matters that seemed better left to case-law development.

Supplemental Rules A, C, E Amended To Conform to G

Rule A. Scope of Rules

(1) These Supplemental Rules apply to:

(A) the procedure in admiralty and maritime claims within the meaning of Rule 9(h) with respect to the following remedies:

(1)(i) maritime attachment and garnishment;

(2)(ii) actions in rem;

(3)(iii) possessory, petitory, and partition actions, and;

(4)(iv) actions for exoneration from or limitation of liability;

(B) forfeiture actions in rem arising from a federal statute; and

(C) These rules also apply to the procedure in statutory condemnation proceedings analogous to maritime actions in rem, whether within the admiralty and maritime jurisdiction or not. Except as otherwise provided, references in these Supplemental Rules to actions in rem include such analogous statutory condemnation proceedings.

(2) The ~~general~~ Federal Rules of Civil Procedure ~~for the United States District Courts are~~ also ~~applicable~~ apply to the foregoing proceedings except to the extent that they are inconsistent with these Supplemental Rules.

Committee Note

Rule A is amended to reflect the adoption of Rule G to govern procedure in civil forfeiture actions. Rule G(1) contemplates application of other Supplemental Rules to the extent that Rule G does not address an issue. One example is the Rule E(4)(c) provision for arresting intangible property.

Rule C. In Rem Actions: Special Provisions

(1) When Available. An action in rem may be brought:

(a) To enforce any maritime lien;

(b) Whenever a statute of the United States provides for a maritime action in rem or a proceeding analogous thereto.

* * * * *

(2) Complaint. In an action in rem the complaint must:

(a) be verified;

(b) describe with reasonable particularity the property that is the subject of the action; and

(c) ~~in an admiralty and maritime proceeding~~ state that the property is within the district or will be within the district while the action is pending;

(d) ~~in a forfeiture proceeding for violation of a federal~~

119

Supplemental Rule C

statute, state:

~~(i) the place of seizure and whether it was on land or on navigable waters;~~

~~(ii) whether the property is within the district, and if the property is not within the district the statutory basis for the court's exercise of jurisdiction over the property; and~~

~~(iii) all allegations required by the statute under which the action is brought.~~

(3) Judicial Authorization and Process.

(a) Arrest Warrant.

~~(i) When the United States files a complaint demanding a forfeiture for violation of a federal statute, the clerk must promptly issue a summons and a warrant for the arrest of the vessel or other property without requiring a certification of exigent circumstances, but if the property is real property the United States must proceed under applicable statutory procedures.~~

~~(ii)~~**(i)**~~(A) In other actions, t~~The court must review the complaint and any supporting papers. If the conditions for an in rem action appear to exist, the court must issue an order directing the clerk to issue a warrant for the arrest of the vessel or other property that is the subject of the action.

~~(B)~~**(ii)** If the plaintiff or the plaintiff's attorney certifies that exigent circumstances make court review impracticable, the clerk must promptly issue a summons and a warrant for the arrest of the vessel or other property that is the subject of the action. The plaintiff has the burden in any ~~postarrest~~ post-arrest hearing under Rule E(4)(f) to show that exigent circumstances existed.

(b) Service.

(i) If the property that is the subject of the action is a vessel or tangible property on board a vessel, the warrant and any supplemental process must be delivered to the marshal for service.

(ii) If the property that is the subject of the action is other property, tangible or intangible, the warrant and any supplemental process must be delivered to a person or organization authorized to enforce it, who may be: (A) a marshal; (B) someone under contract with the United States; (C) someone specially appointed by the court for that purpose; or, (D) in an action brought by the United States, any officer or employee of the United States.

* * * * *

(6) Responsive Pleading; Interrogatories.

~~(a) Civil Forfeiture. In an in rem forfeiture action for violation of a federal statute:~~

~~(i) a person who asserts an interest in or right against the property that is the subject of the action must file a verified statement identifying the interest or right:~~

~~(A) within 30 days after the earlier of (1) the date of service of the Government's complaint or (2) completed publication of notice under Rule C(4), or~~

Supplemental Rule C

<del>(B) within the time that the court allows.</del>

<del>(ii) an agent, bailee, or attorney must state the authority to file a statement of interest in or right against the property on behalf of another; and</del>

<del>(iii) a person who files a statement of interest in or right against the property must serve and file an answer within 20 days after filing the statement.</del>

<del>(b)</del>**(a)** Maritime Arrests and Other Proceedings. <del>In an rem action not governed by Rule C(6)(a):</del>

* * * * *

<del>(c)</del>**(b)** Interrogatories.

* * * * *

Committee Note

Rule C is amended to reflect the adoption of Rule G to govern procedure in civil forfeiture actions.

Rule E. Actions in Rem and Quasi in Rem: General Provisions

* * * * *

(3) Process.

(a) In admiralty and maritime proceedings process in rem or of maritime attachment and garnishment may be served only within the district.

<del>(b) In forfeiture cases process in rem may be served within the district or outside the district when authorized by statute.</del>

<del>(c)</del>**(b)** Issuance and Delivery.

* * * * *

(5) Release of Property.

(a) Special Bond. <del>Except in cases of seizures for for-</del>

~~feiture under any law of the United States, w~~<u>W</u>henever process of maritime attachment and garnishment or process in rem is issued the execution of such process shall be stayed, or the property released, on the giving of security, to be approved by the court or clerk, or by stipulation of the parties, conditioned to answer the judgment of the court or of any appellate court. The parties may stipulate the amount and nature of such security. In the event of the inability or refusal of the parties so to stipulate the court shall fix the principal sum of the bond or stipulation at an amount sufficient to cover the amount of the plaintiff's claim fairly stated with accrued interest and costs; but the principal sum shall in no event exceed (i) twice the amount of the plaintiff's claim or (ii) the value of the property on due appraisement, whichever is smaller. The bond or stipulation shall be conditioned for the payment of the principal sum and interest thereon at 6 per cent per annum.

* * * * *

(9) Disposition of Property; Sales.

~~(a) **Actions for Forfeitures.** In any action in rem to enforce a forfeiture for violation of a statute of the United States the property shall be disposed of as provided by statute.~~

~~(b)~~<u>(a)</u> **Interlocutory Sales; Delivery.**

* * * * *

(**ii**) In the circumstances described in Rule E(9)(<u>a</u>~~b~~)(i), the court, on motion by a defendant or a person filing a statement of interest or right under

Rule C(6), may order that the property, rather than being sold, be delivered to the movant upon giving security under these rules.

~~(c)~~**(b)** **Sales, Proceeds.**

* * * * *

Committee Note

Rule E is amended to reflect the adoption of Rule G to govern procedure in civil forfeiture actions.

Rule 26. General Provisions Governing Discovery; Duty of Disclosure.

(a) Required Disclosures; Methods to Discover Additional Matter.

(1) Initial Disclosures.

* * * * *

(E) The following categories of proceedings are exempt from initial disclosure under Rule 26(a)(1):

* * * * *

(ii) a forfeiture action in rem arising from a federal statute;

~~(ii)~~**(iii)** a petition for habeas corpus or other proceeding to challenge a criminal conviction or sentence;

~~(iii)~~**(iv)** an action brought without counsel by a person in custody of the United States, a state, or a state subdivision;

~~(iv)~~**(v)** an action to enforce or quash an administrative summons or subpoena;

~~(v)~~**(vi)** an action by the United States to recover benefit payments;

(vi)**(vii)** an action by the United States to collect on a student loan guaranteed by the United States;

(vii)**(viii)** a proceeding ancillary to proceedings in other courts; and

(viii)**(ix)** an action to enforce an arbitration award.

* * * * *

Committee Note

Civil forfeiture actions are added to the list of exemptions from Rule 26(a)(1) disclosure requirements. These actions are governed by new Supplemental Rule G. Disclosure is not likely to be useful.

Technical Conforming Amendments, Civil Rules 9(h), 14, 65.1

The process of revising Rule G included conforming amendments to the Supplemental Rules affected by the change, but overlooked the need to conform Civil Rules 9(h) and 65.1 to the new title for the Supplemental Rules and to conform Rules 14(a) and (c) to the changes made in Supplemental Rule C(6). It is recommended that the following technical conforming changes be transmitted to the Judicial Conference for adoption without a period for public comment.

Rule 9. Pleading Special Matters

* * * * *

(h) Admiralty and Maritime Claims. A pleading or count setting forth a claim for relief within the admiralty and maritime jurisdiction that is also within the jurisdiction of the district court on some other ground may contain a statement identifying the claim as an admiralty or maritime claim for the purposes of Rules 14(c), 38(e), and 82, and the Supplemental Rules for Certain Admiralty and or Maritime Claims and Asset Forfeiture Claims. If the claim is cognizable only in admiralty, it is an admiralty or maritime claim for those purposes whether so identified or not. The amendment of a pleading to add or withdraw an identifying statement is governed by the principles of Rule 15. A case that includes an admiralty or maritime claim within this subdivision is an admiralty case within 28 U.S.C. § 1292(a)(3).

Committee Note

Rule 9(h) is amended to conform to the changed title of the Supplemental Rules.

Rule 14. Third-Party Practice
(a) When Defendant May Bring in Third Party.

* * * * *

The third-party complaint, if within the admiralty and maritime jurisdiction, may be in rem against a vessel, cargo, or other property subject to admiralty or maritime process in rem, in which case references in this rule to the summons include the warrant of arrest, and references to the third-party plaintiff or defendant include, where appropriate, a person who asserts a right under Supplemental Rule C(6)(b)(a)(1) in the property arrested.

* * * * *

(c) Admiralty and Maritime Claims.
When a plaintiff asserts an admiralty or maritime claim within the meaning of Rule 9(h), the defendant or person who asserts a right under Supplemental Rule C(6)(b)(a)(1), as a third-party plaintiff, may bring in a third-party defendant who may be wholly or partly liable, either to the plaintiff or to the third-party plaintiff, by way of remedy over, contribution, or otherwise on account of the same transaction, occurrence, or series of

transactions or occurrences. In such a case the third-party plaintiff may also demand judgment against the third-party defendant in favor of the plaintiff, in which event the third-party defendant shall make any defenses to the claim of the plaintiff as well as to that of the third-party plaintiff in the manner provided in Rule 12 and the action shall proceed as if the plaintiff had commenced it against the third-party defendant as well as the third-party plaintiff.

Committee Note

Rule 14 is amended to conform to changes in designating the paragraphs of Supplemental Rule C(6).

Rule 65.1. Security: Proceedings Against Sureties

Whenever these rules, including the Supplemental Rules for ~~Certain~~ Admiralty ~~and~~ or Maritime Claims and Asset Forfeiture Claims, require or permit the giving of security by a party, and security is given in the form of a bond or stipulation or other undertaking with one or more sureties, each surety submits to the jurisdiction of the court and irrevocably appoints the clerk of the court as the surety's agent upon whom any papers affecting the surety's liability on the bond or undertaking may be served. The surety's liability may be enforced on motion without the necessity of an independent action. The motion and such notice of the motion as the court prescribes may be served on the clerk of the court, who shall forthwith mail copies to the sureties if their addresses are known.

Committee Note

Rule 65.1 is amended to conform to the changed title of the supplemental Rules.

127